WICCA SPELLBOOK STARTER KIT

A Book of Candle, Crystal, and Herbal Spells

LISA CHAMBERLAIN

Wicca Spellbook Starter Kit

Published by **Chamberlain Publications (Wicca Shorts)**

ISBN-13: 978-1-912715-47-3

Disclaimer

While all attempts have been made to verify the information provided in this publication, neither the author nor the publisher assumes any responsibility for errors, omissions, or contrary interpretations of the subject matter herein.

This book is for entertainment purposes only. The views expressed are those of the author alone, and should not be taken as expert instruction or commands. The reader is responsible for his or her own actions.

Adherence to all applicable laws and regulations, including international, federal, state, and local governing professional licensing, business practices, advertising, and all other aspects of doing business in the US, Canada, or any other jurisdiction is the sole responsibility of the purchaser or reader.

Neither the author nor the publisher assumes any responsibility or liability whatsoever on the behalf of the purchaser or reader of these materials.

Any perceived slight of any individual or organization is purely unintentional.

YOUR FREE GIFT

Thank you for adding this book to your Wiccan library! To learn more, why not join Lisa's Wiccan community and get an exclusive, free spell book?

The book is a great starting point for anyone looking to try their hand at practicing magic. The ten beginner-friendly spells can help you to create a positive atmosphere within your home, protect yourself from negativity, and attract love, health, and prosperity.

Little Book of Spells is now available to read on your laptop, phone, tablet, Kindle or Nook device!

To download, simply visit the following link:

GET THREE FREE AUDIOBOOKS FROM LISA CHAMBERLAIN

INTRODUCTION

Welcome to the *Wicca Spellbook Starter Kit*. Together, these three collections of spells, rituals, magical charms, and recipes form a comprehensive grimoire of accessible, practical magic to inspire and help you develop your own unique practice.

Each Book of Shadows in this set expands on a form of magic covered in my three beginner guides, *Candle Magic, Crystal Magic,* and *Herbal Magic*. The 160 magical workings within are designed for beginners and more advanced practitioners alike.

Book of Candle Spells focuses on working with the Element of Fire, and the potent vibrational frequencies of the visible light spectrum. Candles take center stage to varying degrees across the collection—some spells are focused exclusively on the combined magic of candle and color, while others incorporate additional tools such as crystals and other color-appropriate ingredients. The spells are also organized by color, with chapter introductions detailing the magical properties and uses for the 14 colors most widely used in Wiccan and other contemporary magic.

Book of Crystal Spells is devoted to the magical uses of the 13 crystals and other mineral stones introduced in *Crystal Magic*. Many of these spells are focused on aspects of emotional healing and energetic balancing, two purposes that crystals are uniquely suited for, but you'll also find more traditional goals represented, like prosperity, protection, and relationships. The spells are organized by stone, rather than by purpose, so you can develop a magical connection with different types of crystals, one at a time. You'll find an overview of the properties of each stone in the chapter introductions.

Likewise, *Book of Herbal Spells* takes the information from *Herbal Magic* to the next level, with a chapter for each of the 13 herbs featured in the original book. Single herbs are often the main focus of these spells, with minimal additional ingredients, to help you deepen your own magical relationships with the subtle energies of the herbs themselves. As you work more and more with herbal magic, you will develop a natural affinity with these marvelous plant beings that have been co-creating with magical people since the beginning of time.

I hope that you find many useful workings, and plenty of inspiration, in these three collections. As I always say in all of my books, follow your own inner guidance as you browse through the spells and read about the magical properties of colors, crystals, and herbs.

Feel free to tailor any spell to your individual approach to magic—add or substitute ingredients, compose your own spell words to replace those suggested here, or even just borrow the form and structure of a spell to use for a different purpose, with different ingredients. And if you're the kind of person who likes to follow a spell exactly as written, this time-honored approach works just as well—as long as you resonate with every detail of it. Your magical methods are entirely up to you!

Here's to continued learning and growth along your path, and to the magical gifts granted to us all through the abundant generosity of our beloved Earth.

Enjoy your journey, and Blessed Be!

OVERVIEW

The *Spellbook Starter Kit* consists of the following three books:

WICCA BOOK OF CANDLE SPELLS

A Beginner's Book of Shadows for Wiccans, Witches, and Other Practitioners of Candle Magic

LISA CHAMBERLAIN

CONTENTS

INTRODUCTION

Welcome to my *Book of Candle Spells!*

Candle magic brings together two powerful sources of magical energy: the Element of Fire and the potent vibrations of color magic. Candle magic is widely recognized as the easiest form of magic for beginners to work with, as it is quite accessible and highly effective. Of course, seasoned magicians also still find candle spells rewarding, and this book is designed to bring new ideas to your magical practice no matter your level of experience.

Candles take center stage to varying degrees across this collection—some are focused exclusively on the combined magic of candle and color, while others incorporate additional tools such as crystals and other color-oriented ingredients. The spells are organized by color, and feature the 14 colors most widely used in Wiccan and other contemporary magic. You can personalize the spells by choosing your own preferred shades of any given color, if you like.

The spells in this book call for a variety of candle types. Many use spell candles, which are well-sized for single-use workings and available in Wiccan and occult-oriented shops, as well as online. Other spells call for pillar candles, which are longer-lasting and tend to be safer and sturdier than other candles. Tea lights and votives are easy to handle and work well in spells calling for multiple candles and outdoor workings.

Occasionally, a spell will call for a taper candle, which can be messy in terms of dripping wax, but this can be a nice enhancement of the magical atmosphere desired for spellwork. Many spells will call for "work candles," which are simply used to bring the mind into a more magical focus as the spellwork begins. These can be any size, and are always an option in any working, but are noted in the ingredients lists here when they're particularly helpful.

Some candle colors are more widely available than others, and depending on your access to magical supply shops, it might be more difficult to find certain colors. If need be, a white candle can be substituted for these colors, as will be discussed in the White chapter.

Many people wonder what to do with the unused portions of their candles after the spellwork is complete. Several spells call for letting the candle burn out on its own, but if you are instructed to extinguish the candle, you may use it again for atmosphere (just don't use it for other workings).

On occasion, disposal of the candle may be called for, if the working is for removal of negative energy. Traditionally, this is done by burying the candle, although some ecologically-minded Witches prefer not to disturb any life within the soil with a human-made object. This is entirely up to you, so do what your intuition advises. If you do choose to throw candle remnants in the trash, do so with an attitude of ceremony, rather than mindlessly tossing your magical leftovers in the bin.

When it comes to extinguishing candles, this is ideally done with a candle snuffer or by waving your hands over the flame, rather than blowing it out. If you do need to blow it out, just make a point of thanking the Element of Fire for its role in the spell before doing to. As for what to light your candles with, opinions abound on whether matches or a lighter is better for magical work. Use your intuition (or whatever you happen to have on hand!) in this regard as well.

Anointing candles with magically-charged oils is a time-honored tradition in Witchcraft, and many spells in this book call for the use of essential oils for this purpose. Most will offer a few different choices of oils, based on their magical correspondences. You are free, of course, to create your own blend using a combination of these and/or other oils, or use a tried-and-true blend you already work with, if it's sufficiently related to the purpose of the spell.

Do be aware of the amount of oil on your fingertips before lighting the candle, as oil is flammable! Wash or wipe your hands after anointing, if necessary. You can find more information about anointing candles and working magic with essential oils in my books *Candle Magic* and *Essential Oils Magic.*

As always, each spell in this book assumes that you have already energetically cleared and charged all ingredients prior to beginning the work. Charging candles can be as easy as holding them between your palms and sending your focused energy into the wax, or placing them on a consecrated pentacle slab. Depending on your practice, you might invoke the Goddess and God, the Elements, or other spiritual energies you work with to aid you in your magic. If you haven't yet learned to charge magical items, research and try a few different methods until you find what feels most appropriate for you.

Each spell also assumes you have done your part to bring yourself into a magically-focused state of mind, as this is the most important aspect of the work. This is a highly individualized process for each practitioner, but usually involves some kind of meditation or other relaxation technique. Many of these spells include reminders to spend time quieting your mind, but it's up to you to take this step before any magical working. It is ultimately *your* energy that's shifting the reality of the Universe, so shape it well and use it wisely!

Finally, while the words provided in these spells are effective at sealing the work, they are meant to be taken as suggestions only. If they resonate with you, then by all means use them! However, please feel free to substitute words of your own choosing, as this adds an extra element of your own unique magical power to the work.

It is my hope that you find many inspiring and useful spells among this candle-oriented collection. As always, remember that you are the magician, and any additions, subtractions, or other alterations to the spells that occur to you are worth trying, as long as they resonate with your own inner guide. Enjoy your continuing exploration of the world of candle and color magic!

Blessed Be.

RED

We all know red as the first color of the rainbow, but it is also among the most potent colors used in magic. It is not by any means a "neutral" color, and can provoke strong impressions, both positive and negative, depending on its context.

On the one hand, red roses are symbolic of love and passion, and are generally thought to be pleasing by those who give and receive them. On the other hand, the phrase "seeing red" describes feelings of anger and rage. Red is not a subtle color, to say the least!

At the most basic physical level, red relates to survival. It is the color of blood and of a healthy human heart. Red is also associated with the root chakra, which relates to issues of instinct, safety, survival, and boundaries. As such, red is associated with vitality and strength, good health, and the will to do what is necessary to survive and thrive.

This color is appropriate for magic related to physical healing and raising one's physical energy, as well as to motivation, willpower, ambition, and determination. Anything that contributes to basic security, such as business deals, career goals, or the acquisition of a home can benefit from red's magical energies. Red can also assist with issues requiring courage, fast action, leadership, and strength. It helps with confidence and self-esteem, and can help increase your personal vibrancy so that you stand out in a group.

Red's very masculine energy can be harnessed for workings related to lust and male sexual potency, as well as matters involving conflict or competition. Yet this color is also associated with the energies of joy, birth, celebration and renewal. And of course, red is the quintessential color of passion—whether related to romance, sex, a favorite hobby or pursuit, a social cause, or anything else you feel passionate about.

Red candles can add a "quickening" power to spellwork in general, but are particularly potent in spellwork related to any of the matters listed above. Red is a color of Fire and can be used in ritual to represent this Element. Astrologically, red is associated with the signs of Aries and Scorpio and the planet Mars. Its cardinal direction is South.

The spells in this chapter are aimed at helping you attract a passionate lover into your life, boost your physical energy, improve your health, and fire up your willpower to complete a challenging task.

PASSIONATE RELATIONSHIP SPELL

When you're ready for a new lover, don't just cast a general "love spell" without taking some time to consider what you really want out of a relationship. Otherwise, your powerful magic may bring you more of the same types of people you've already moved on from.

So take some time to clearly define what it is you're looking for. You may want to prepare a list of qualities that you desire in a lover ahead of time, since you'll be writing and speaking about them during the spell.

Of course, a truly healthy, passionate relationship must involve self-esteem and self-appreciation in both partners, so you'll also be focusing on yourself in this spell. Spend some time affirming for yourself the positive qualities that you have to bring to a new relationship so that you have them clearly in mind as you begin the work.

<u>You will need:</u>

- 1 red spell candle
- Cinnamon, jasmine, or rose essential oil
- Crystal point, athame, or other ritual carving tool
- White paper
- Red pencil or marker
- Scissors

- Wax paper

Instructions:

Carve a heart shape or other symbol of love into the candle, and anoint it with the oil. Now light the candle, and allow the wax to begin melting.

Meanwhile, cut two heart shapes, about the size of your palms, out of the paper.

Using the red pencil or marker, take one of the hearts and write the most important qualities you seek in a romantic partner. On the other heart, write a list of qualities you have to offer to another.

Hold the hearts in your hands for a moment as you focus on bringing new love into your life.

Now, place the hearts so that they overlap each other on a sheet of wax paper. Speaking out loud, take turns listing the qualities written on each heart.

As you list each one, drip a few drops of wax onto the hearts to seal them together. When you have finished speaking and the hearts are sealed, say the following (or similar) words:

"Passionate hearts, passionate minds,
Passionate souls, we now entwine.
So let it be."

Place the hearts on your altar or in a special space in your home. Allow the candle to burn out on its own.

SUNLIGHT RITUAL FOR PHYSICAL ENERGY

This spell draws on the color red's connection to the Sun and the Element of Fire. The Sun is the source of virtually all energy on our planet. This makes it the most obvious source to work with when you need to boost your physical energy!

As you perform this ritual, know that thousands of others across the world and throughout the span of human history, are with you. Cultures around the world, from the Aztecs to the Hindus to the ancient Egyptians to many Native American cultures revere the Sun in some way. It is an ageless tradition, offered here with a modern approach.

Ideally, this ritual is performed outside in direct sunlight on flat ground. However, you can create a vivid visualization of the Sun if you feel the need to work on a cloudy day, or work with bright lamplight and/or several large candles. All additional candles should be either red, yellow, orange, white, or pink.

<u>You will need:</u>

- 3 red candles
- Sunshine
- Work candle(s) for atmosphere (if working without direct sunlight)
- 3 large squares of tinfoil

<u>Instructions:</u>

Before the ritual, place one red candle (in a safe, sturdy holder) on each piece of tin foil. Arrange them on flat ground in a triangle shape, with enough space to stand in the center of the triangle.

Step inside the triangle and light the candles. Focus on the light of the candles and the sunlight bouncing off of the foil. Close your eyes, place your palms upward, and feel the warmth of the Sun on your skin.

With your eyes still closed, visualize the power of the Sun and the light of the candles filling your body with positive energy. See it start at your toes and work its way up until it reaches the top of your head.

Open your eyes and take a moment to feel the fullness of the solar energy inside of you. Say a word or two of thanks to the Sun for its never-ending energy and sustaining light.

Extinguish the candles and recycle the foil or save to use again when you repeat the ritual.

HEALING FIRE REGENERATION SPELL

Fire magic is excellent for banishing, and red's association with both Fire and health makes it the perfect choice for ridding yourself of a health issue. This spell honors the role of Fire in the forest—the destruction of the old in order to make room for the new. You will be "burning away" an old, unwanted physical form in order to bring in the new, healed, version of yourself.

Bay leaves are associated with healing and the fulfillment of wishes. What's more, burning a bay leaf in the home has been shown to relieve anxiety and boost the immune system!

As with any magic, this spell is not meant to replace needed medical care. However, it will certainly add power to any healing process initiated by a medical professional. And while your health issue may not be resolved overnight, you will be aligning yourself with healing vibrational frequencies, allowing the process to unfold at a much faster rate than it would otherwise.

Depending on the size of your bay leaf and fireproof bowl, you may want to keep a small amount of water on hand just to be on the safe side. If you don't have a red pencil, a regular pencil is fine.

You will need:

- 1 red spell candle
- 1 bay leaf
- 1 red pencil
- Small fireproof bowl
- Small cup of water (optional)

Instructions:

Before you begin, take three deep breaths and focus your energy on a white light radiating from your heart center. During each exhale, feel the light washing away any negativity or anxiety and allow your muscles to relax. When you feel calm, clear, and focused, light the red candle.

On the bay leaf, write down the health issue you're seeking to banish. Then spend a few minutes visualizing your body as you wish it to be.

For example, if you have an injured knee, visualize walking, running, jumping, etc. with two completely healthy and pain-free knees. If you have a cold, visualize breathing freely and having plenty of energy. Hold and strengthen this vision for a few moments.

When you feel ready, say the following (or similar) words:

"I release all imbalances of body, mind, and soul.
This fire of regeneration makes me whole.
It is done."

Now light the bay leaf on fire with the candle flame, and drop it into the dish to burn completely. (If the fire goes out before the leaf has completely burned, you can carefully relight it, either with the candle flame or a match.)

Allow the candle to burn out on its own. Scatter the ashes of the bay leaf over the Earth.

WILL-POWERED VICTORY CHARM

Whether you're trying to incorporate a new exercise routine, give up an unwanted habit, clean out your basement, or conquer some other daunting task, the fiery energy of red will help you summon the will to get started and the drive to succeed.

Red jasper, a mineral stone revered for its grounding and strengthening properties, makes an excellent magical charm for this purpose, but you can use any red stone if need be.

You will need:

- 1 red pillar candle
- Crystal point, athame, or other ritual carving tool
- 1 piece of red jasper or other red stone
- Anointing oil (optional)

Instructions:

Carve a symbol appropriate to your goal into the candle. This can be a "V" for victory, a runic symbol with a similar meaning, a pentacle, or even your initials—whatever symbol holds power for you related to this particular magical goal.

Anoint the candle with the oil, if using.

Now hold the red jasper or other stone between your palms.

Close your eyes, take a deep breath, and envision yourself succeeding at your task. Enjoy the feeling of victory and the pride of self-accomplishment.

When you feel ready, place the stone in front of the candle.

Light the candle as you say the following (or similar) words three times:

"I am energy. I am willpower. I am success. I am worthy."

When the candle has burned out on its own, your victory charm is charged and ready to assist you. Keep it with you whenever willpower is needed to accomplish your goal.

ORANGE

The upbeat energies of orange are a blend of red and yellow energies. The influence of red brings the properties of strength, stamina, vitality and ambition, while yellow contributes energies of cheerful encouragement, confidence, and optimism.

Orange is useful in magic related to both physical concerns, such as boosting energy and personal power, and concerns of the mind, such as acquiring needed information, improving memory, or summoning mental agility in a challenging situation. As a color of sunrise and sunset, orange is both powerful and peaceful, promoting balance and a sense of warmth and well-being. And like the popular fruit that bears its name, orange is sustaining and rejuvenating.

Orange is associated with the sacral chakra, which governs creativity, movement, change, and emotions. The vibrations of orange can dispel depression, grief, feelings of abandonment, and other negative emotional energies, and help manage strong emotions. Orange also promotes joy, kindness, happiness, sharing, and an eagerness to have fun. It aids with social communication, and the ability to adapt smoothly to sudden change.

Orange is a color of Fire and can be used in solar magic, but its yellow-based energy also links it to the Element of Air. Accordingly, its cardinal direction can be either South or East. Astrologically, orange is associated with the Sun, the planets Mercury and Mars, and the signs of Leo and Sagittarius.

Orange is also a color of the harvest, and can be used in spells to bring forth the positive results of your recent efforts, especially when related to careers, promotions, and business. Orange brings success in legal matters, especially related to investments and to selling property, such as a home. It is also used to call in new opportunities in any of these areas.

The spells below work with orange candles and other orange ingredients to assist with adapting to change, raising your vibration through self-encouragement, strengthening your sense of empowerment, and boosting your vitality.

SPELL FOR NAVIGATING SUDDEN CHANGE

Change is often startling and uncomfortable. This is true whether the change is positive, negative, expected, or unexpected. When it comes to unexpected change, however, it's very common to get thrown off-balance by the disruption it causes. Yet all change brings with it new possibilities for improved circumstances, no matter how counterintuitive that may seem at the time.

This spell can help you navigate the choppy waters of unexpected change by shifting your perspective on the situation and rebalancing your energy, opening you up to receive unexpected blessings.

You will need:

- 1 orange pillar candle
- Orange or bergamot essential oil
- Oil burner or diffuser
- Journal or writing paper

Instructions:

Heat the oil in the burner or diffuser and then spend a few moments breathing deeply to quiet your mind.

When you feel grounded and centered, light the pillar candle and begin to freewrite about the situation.

Start by identifying the change that has happened, and then write about what you liked about the way things were before.

Spend some time envisioning what positive developments are possible now that this change has occurred. You don't need to know *how* these developments might come about—simply open your mind to the potential that this sudden change has made possible.

For example, if you've just lost a job, imagine what new and better opportunities could be coming your way. If you had travel plans that have fallen through, imagine what you can do with the time and money that have just been freed up.

Be creative and intuitive with your freewriting, rather than logical or analytical. Write for at least fifteen minutes total. As you write, imagine the candle shining a bright orange light upon you and surrounding you in its energetic field.

When you're finished, fold up the pages you've written and place them next to the candle. As you do so, say the following (or similar) words:

"Winds of change are the breath of life.
I am grounded, centered, and ready for new blessings.
So let it be."

Place the candle in a special place in your home and know that you can light it whenever you need some extra support during this time of change.

When some time has passed and you've adjusted to the change, you may want to revisit your freewriting to see how you have shifted since working the spell.

ENCOURAGEMENT SPELL FOR CHALLENGING TIMES

When faced with a difficult situation, whether it's a challenging task, a tough life transition, or simply a garden-variety case of "the blues," the vibrational frequencies of orange can be immensely helpful to your ability to overcome negative emotions. This spell will help you bring in the support you need by affirming what you are currently doing, honoring the character traits you admire in yourself, and encouraging an optimistic outlook.

You should shoot for as many encouraging notes as you can, but use a minimum of seven. If you can't find orange sticky notes, white or yellow will work just as well.

Note: because you will be leaving paper in close proximity to a burning candle, it's best not to leave the spell candle unattended at all. If this isn't possible, then gently extinguish the spell candle when the work is finished, and feel free to relight it along with the pillar candle at a later stage.

You will need:

- 1 orange spell candle
- 1 orange pillar candle
- Bergamot essential oil (optional)
- Several (at least 7) orange sticky notes

Instructions:

Anoint the spell candle with the oil, if using. Light the pillar candle and take a few moments to quiet your mind. Allow for the possibility of positive thoughts to flow into your experience.

When you're ready, begin to write messages of encouragement to yourself, using one sticky note for each message. For best results, focus on three categories: giving support to where you are in this moment, honoring what makes you feel good about yourself, and affirming an optimistic viewpoint.

Some examples of words of encouragement are "I am exactly where I'm supposed to be," "I am a kind person," and "I always rise to meet my challenges."

Write as many as you can, but make sure you agree with each statement you're making. If seven is all you can manage, that's perfectly fine!

Arrange the messages around the orange spell candle in a circle, reading each one aloud before you place it down. Visualize the power of the words giving you a boost of encouragement.

When you feel your energy begin to lift, light the spell candle as you say the following (or similar) words:

"Every positive word I say
brings more light and joy my way.
And so it is."

If you can, allow the spell candle to burn out on its own. Place the sticky notes in various spots around your home, your car, or wherever else you will see them often.

You can continue to relight the orange pillar candle (as well as the spell candle, if need be) whenever you would like to reactivate the encouraging vibrations.

EMPOWERING ORANGE BATH SPELL

Ritual baths are often used for purification, calming, and healing purposes, but you can also use bath magic to promote more masculine energies like confidence and ambition.

If you're facing a challenge or situation that has you feeling uneasy, try this vibration-shifting spell, using orange's dual energies of peace and strength to dispel negative feelings and help you tap into your personal power. This is a great spell to do the night before an exam, a difficult conversation with a coworker or employer, or any other situation where you need to be both sharp and composed.

You will need:

- 1 orange candle
- Other candles for atmosphere (optional)
- 1-2 tablespoons dried orange peels
- 3-7 drops orange essential oil

Instructions:

Run a warm bath to begin the ritual.

When the tub is full, add the orange essential oil and scatter the dried orange peels over the water. Light the orange candle and any other atmosphere candles, and turn off any artificial lighting.

Gently enter the bath and breathe deeply, allowing the scent of the orange oil to envelop you. Take a few deep breaths, focusing only on your inhalation and exhalation. Note the shift in your personal energy as you continue to relax.

Now imagine the situation or challenge you are wanting to be empowered for. See yourself speaking and acting in a manner that you are completely satisfied with. Summon whatever it is you want to feel about the situation once it has passed.

When you have a strong hold on the feeling, take a deep breath in, and visualize orange light suffusing your entire body. On the exhale, release your vision and all further thought on the matter.

Take some time to enjoy the rest of your bath, and when you're ready, emerge from the tub, dry off, and gently extinguish the candle(s).

JUICY SUNSHINE VITALITY SPELL

We all know that orange juice is good for you, but like any food, the nutritional properties of an orange can be magnified and energized by adding in some magic!

If you've been feeling depleted of energy, or if you just want to try a fun experiment with kitchen witchery, grab some oranges and a knife (you can use your athame for this if you like) and get ready for a sunny boost of energy!

You may want to work this spell in your kitchen, as it can be a little messy for altar work, but this is entirely up to you.

You will need:

- 3 orange candles
- 3 oranges

- Knife
- Cup

Instructions:

Place the three candles a few inches apart on your altar or kitchen table, and place one orange in front of each candle.

Slice the first orange in half, and set the two halves back in front of the candle. Then light the candle as you say the following (or similar) words:

"I thank the Sun for its life-giving light."

Repeat this process with the other two oranges. When lighting the second candle, say:

"I thank the Sun for its loving warmth."

When lighting the third candle, say:

"I thank the Sun for its sustaining energy."

Then take the halves of the first orange and squeeze their juice into the cup, focusing on the power and energy of the orange collecting in your cup through the light of the candle flame. Repeat this with the other two oranges.

When you have squeezed all the juice out of the oranges, take a moment to hold the cup in your hands. Take a deep breath in, letting the refreshing scent and the bright candle light wash positive energy over you.

Each time you take a sip of the orange juice say an affirmation like "I am filled with physical and mental energy." When you've finished the juice, gently extinguish the candles and enjoy your increased vitality!

YELLOW

The cheerful, sunny energies of yellow are known for having instant vibration-raising effects on those who simply gaze at the color for a few moments.

Yellow is actually the brightest color on the spectrum, and its harmonious energy helps us move away from the lower vibrations of stress and sadness. Yellow helps us open our capacity to enjoy the present moment, making way to experience optimism, happiness, and joy.

Yellow is primarily associated with the functions of the intellect, and is used in magic relating to memory, concentration, focus, and general mental clarity. It is the ideal magical color for students, as it assists with not merely acquiring knowledge, but truly understanding the subject matter one is studying. Yellow can help dissolve mental blocks and even accelerate the learning process, which is handy whether you're taking a class, training for a new job, or simply taking up a new hobby.

As a color of the Air Element, yellow is also used in spellwork related to creative intelligence— imagination, inspiration, ingenuity, and new ideas—in both the arts and the business realm. Draw on the power of yellow when you feel stuck in a creative project or need to contribute original ideas to a group endeavor. If you're seeking improved communication with friends or colleagues, or want to enhance your skills of persuasion, yellow is the ideal magical ally. Yellow is also used in spellwork related to travel—especially air travel—as well as intuition, divination, astral projection, and communicating with beings in the spirit realm.

Yellow also boosts self-awareness, self-esteem, and confidence, and is associated with the solar chakra, which governs these qualities. It is used in spellwork related to healing, pleasure, flexibility, beauty, and friendship. Yellow is also associated with the Sun as well as the planet Mercury, and the signs of Taurus and Libra. Its cardinal direction is East. As a Sun color, it is good for spells and rituals that call specifically on solar energies or deities associated with the Sun.

The magical workings below include a scrying session using the color yellow, spellwork focused on enhancing communication and boosting your self-confidence, and a "study buddy" in the form of an enchanted yellow candle.

COLOR SCRYING RITUAL

Scrying is an ancient and versatile form of divination, using water, crystal balls, tea leaves, and even cloud forms to reveal images and information not normally available to the conscious mind. But it isn't an art that comes easily to everyone.

This fun method uses the interaction between water and color to allow for more readily-seen images to come through, which works well as a beginning scrying exercise. For best results, try this at night by candlelight!

Yellow's association with the Element of Air and with divination makes it a great color to work with here, both in terms of the water and the candle(s). You may wish to approach this ritual with a specific question in mind, or simply be open to whatever images and impressions come through.

The food coloring will eventually dissolve into the water, but if you begin with cold water, you should have plenty of time for scrying before this happens.

<u>You will need:</u>

- 1 yellow spell candle
- Anointing oil (optional)
- Work candles for atmosphere (optional)
- Small bowl

- Cup of cold water
- Yellow food coloring
- Journal or writing paper (optional)

Instructions:

Find a quiet place to sit where you will be able to gaze into the bowl of water, ideally with the yellow candle(s) directly behind the bowl.

Anoint the spell candle with the oil, if using. Light any atmosphere candles and then spend a few moments quieting your mind. You may wish to think of a specific question at this time, but it's not necessary.

When you feel ready, open your eyes and light the yellow candle. You can state your question at this time, or simply affirm that you're open to helpful communication from the invisible realms.

Now pour the cup of water into the small bowl.

Train your focus on the water, emptying your mind of any other thoughts. Hold the bottle of food coloring about a foot above the bowl and squeeze three drops into the water.

With a soft gaze and receptive state of mind, sit quietly and allow any impressions from the yellow swirls within the water to arise in your consciousness. You may want to occasionally give the water a brief, gentle swirl with your finger to create more movement.

Feel free to write down any images, ideas, revelations, etc. that come to you during this exercise.

When you're finished, or when the food coloring has dissolved into the water completely, gently extinguish the spell candle and pour the water down the sink.

CONFIDENT COMMUNICATION SPELL

Many Witches and other magical practitioners find themselves to be the "odd one out" in group settings, whether it's at work, at school, or even among social acquaintances. Sometimes the gap between what we know of the Universe and how it is perceived through the lenses of "Muggles" is so great that we're afraid to open our mouths, lest we say something "weird" and create an awkward moment.

While you may never be able to open up someone else's mind to the hidden, magical underpinnings of reality, you should still feel free to speak your mind about any topic from your own unique perspective.

Yellow's airy and cheerful frequencies make it a great color to work with in this regard, as it fosters clear communication and a sunny aura at the same time. Those in your social sphere will be able to hear your words in whatever way makes the most sense for them, without discomfort or confusion causing conflict between you.

Most importantly, you will feel confident and secure within yourself, and not worried about what anyone else thinks about what you're saying!

<u>You will need:</u>

- 3 yellow votives or tea lights
- Bergamot, cinnamon, clove, or lemon essential oil (optional)

<u>Instructions:</u>

Anoint the candles with the oil, if using.

Arrange the candles in a line on your altar or workspace. The candle to the left represents you, and the candle to the right represents your "audience," or the people you come into contact with in your daily life. The candle in the middle represents your communications to others.

Light the first candle and say the following (or similar) words:

"I am a sovereign being, in tune with the workings of the Universe."

Light the middle candle and say the following (or similar) words:

"I speak with clarity, honesty, and integrity in all of my interactions."

Now light the third candle and say the following (or similar) words:

"My words are heard by those with ears to hear, hearts to feel, and minds to understand."

Allow the candles to burn for at least an hour, or all the way out on their own.

If you like, you can repeat this spell for each social context you move through in your daily life: work, school, friends, family, etc.

MIRROR MAGIC FOR SELF-ESTEEM

Everyone experiences challenges in the self-esteem department from time to time. This spell is designed for anyone who wants to feel good about themselves on a regular basis. And if you struggle with self-esteem to the point that you don't like looking in the mirror, then this spell is definitely for you!

Yellow's bright, harmonious energies of self-awareness, confidence, and encouragement can help you retrain your mind away from negative, unhelpful thoughts about yourself and toward more healing, positive, productive thoughts instead.

A large mounted mirror is ideal for this working, but a smaller mirror will also work—it just needs to rest securely against something so that you can write on it.

<u>You will need:</u>

- 1 yellow votive or tea light
- Work candle(s) for atmosphere (optional)
- Mirror
- Yellow Expo or other erasable marker

Instructions:

Light any atmosphere candles, and place the yellow candle so that you can see its reflection in the mirror.

Close your eyes and spend a few moments breathing deeply and quieting your mind.

When you feel ready, light the yellow candle and look directly at yourself in the mirror. Using the yellow non-permanent marker, begin to write adjectives and phrases that describe all of your positive qualities.

For example, you could write words such as "friendly, caring, thoughtful, articulate, intelligent," etc. You can identify talents and skills that you're proud of, or even write about past accomplishments that you're still proud of. Be creative in assessing all of your best characteristics!

However, be sure that you believe these things about yourself, at least some of the time. In other words, if you feel your heart sinking as you write a word because you don't think it's true, then you're putting negative energy into the spell and severely reducing its effectiveness. So if you've always loved baseball, but truly aren't skilled at it, don't write "good at baseball." Instead, write something like "good at loving baseball!"

Cover the mirror with as many words and phrases as you can. When you're finished writing, take a moment to read the words you have written. Repeat them out loud as you look into your own eyes in the mirror.

Close your eyes and take a deep breath, internalizing the positive vibrations of the words and their yellow color. Exhale and open your eyes, gazing at yourself in the mirror a final time.

Leave the candle near the mirror to burn out on its own. You can leave the words up on your mirror to read each day, or take a photo of the work to print and place on your altar before wiping the mirror clean.

YELLOW "STUDY BUDDY" SPELL

If you have an important test coming up, a class presentation in which you really need to shine, or even such a burdensome number of class assignments that you don't know where to start, try this creative, hands-on spell. Yellow's airy, intellectual energies will physically merge with the academic material you're working with and bring you into the ultimate "study flow."

Ideally this spell is worked with an actual textbook, folder, or binder that you use for your class, but if this isn't applicable, you can use any book or other study material as a representation of your task.

<u>You will need:</u>

- 1 yellow pillar candle
- Peppermint, clary sage, or bergamot essential oil
- Several feet of yellow ribbon
- Scissors
- Textbook or binder

<u>Instructions:</u>

Anoint the candle with the oil as you visualize yourself assimilating new information, sparking new ideas, and moving from task to task with ease.

Light the candle and allow the wax to melt for a while until a small pool has gathered. Meanwhile, wrap a piece of yellow ribbon vertically around the front cover of the textbook or binder.

When the wax is ready, cut the ribbon to overlap just a bit and seal the ends of the ribbon together by dripping a small bead of wax on one end. Repeat this with the back cover of the textbook or binder.

Hold the enchanted book or binder in your hands and say the following (or similar) words three times:

"My mind is sharp, focused, and ready. I learn with each new breath."

Now cut several 8-inch pieces of ribbon that you can then use as bookmarks or placeholders while you are studying. Place the candle, bookmarks, and study materials in your study area and get to work!

GREEN

Green is a color widely associated with the season of spring and the bursting forth of new life. It is the color of grass, leaves, and plant life in general, and is used in magic associated with the fairy realm.

Containing the energies of both yellow and blue, this vibrant color is both healing and uplifting, and its masculine and feminine energies evoke a sense of balance and harmony. As the color of the heart chakra, green is a mediator between the realm of thought and the realm of emotion, and assists in workings related to compassion, love (including love of self) and healthy partnerships, including marriages.

In the magical world, green is perhaps best known as the color of abundance and good luck. In fact, it is the predominant color of paper money in the United States, which gave rise to the slang term "green" in reference to cash. Green is indeed used in spellwork related to increasing financial well-being, but it's also very effective for any kind of abundance, whether it's good health, supportive friends and family, or a farm or garden ripe with nourishing crops.

Green is also associated with the related concept of prosperity—a reliable, continuous source of well-being as opposed to a one-time boon of good fortune. As such, green is also excellent for workings related to employment or career matters, the growth of business, and positive returns on investments.

Green's association with the flourishing of plant life makes it an ideal color for spellwork focused on physical fertility, as well as all kinds of renewal, rebirth, rejuvenation, and transformation. It is a color of new beginnings, and can be used to support personal growth and progress toward any goal. Of course, green is highly appropriate for magic related to gardening, gaining skills in herbal healing, preservation of trees and other plant life, and environmental concerns.

Green is a color of Earth and can be used in magic and rituals to represent this Element. Astrologically, it is associated with the planets Venus, Jupiter, Mars, and Mercury, and with the signs of Aquarius, Cancer, and Taurus. Its cardinal direction is North.

The spells in this chapter utilize green candles to boost your financial prosperity, help you gain rewarding employment, increase chances of conceiving a child, and promote good luck.

MAGIC CASH SPELL

There are many spells out there that involve charging actual cash—either coins or paper bills—to attract more cash. This version draws very directly from the power of the green spell candle, with a little help from prosperous patchouli oil.

<u>You will need:</u>

- 1 green spell candle
- Patchouli essential oil
- 1 five-dollar bill
- Green rubber band

<u>Instructions:</u>

Anoint the candle with the patchouli oil.

Fold the five-dollar bill in half lengthwise and wrap it around the candle.

Secure the bill with the rubber band, leaving at least an inch of space between the bill and the candle wick so that the flame will not ignite the bill.

Now hold the wrapped candle between your palms and summon up the feeling of being flush with cash, with all of your basic needs met and the ability to spend some money on yourself!

When you have a solid hold on this feeling, say the following (or similar) words three times:

"As above, so below.
So money in my life does flow.
Land to sky, shore to shore,
this money brings me money more."

Light the candle and allow it to burn down to the top of the five-dollar bill.

Gently extinguish the candle, and when the wax has cooled, unwrap the bill. Carry it with you in your wallet, but don't spend it—instead, whenever you see it, remind yourself that you are attracting more cash into your life each day.

LUCKY PENNY EMPLOYMENT SPELL

Job hunting is one of those tasks where our personal energy makes all the difference—not just at the interview, but in every step leading up to it. Being confident that you will find a well-paying job that you actually like greatly increases your chances of manifesting this outcome.

This spell allows you to focus the positive energy of your grandest desires into a physical talisman that you can carry with you throughout the job-seeking process—including to that final interview!

If you're concerned about protecting the surface of your altar or work space from any spilled candle wax, you might want to place a small piece of wax paper under the coin.

You will need:

- 1 green spell candle
- Patchouli, clove, lavender, or bergamot essential oil
- 1 new penny
- Wax paper (optional)
- Journal or writing paper (optional)

Instructions:

Anoint both sides of the penny with the oil, and then place it face-up on your altar or table, in front of the spell candle.

Light the spell candle and, as the wax begins to melt, spend several minutes focusing on how you will feel once you're working in your new ideal job.

For extra powerful magic, freewrite for awhile on the characteristics of the job you wish to manifest.

When you feel a strong sense of satisfaction with your vision, and when enough wax has melted, carefully tip the candle to drip three drops of green wax onto the coin. As you do so, say the following (or similar) words:

"The job is mine. It is done."

Return the candle to its holder and allow it to burn out on its own. Once it's out, keep the coin with you in your pocket or purse as you go out and find your ideal new job.

CANDLELIGHT FERTILITY SPELL

For women struggling to conceive a child, much assistance can be found from herbal medicine, acupuncture, and modern medical treatments. In conjunction with whatever you are currently trying, this simple spell can help create the vibrational atmosphere necessary for conception to occur.

Because fertility and conception are such personal undertakings, the symbol you carve into the candle should be chosen by you. If you aren't familiar with any fertility symbols, do some research (there are many, many options from cultures around the world to choose from) or create your own.

In preparation for this spell, be sure to take some time to quiet your mind, breathe deeply, and let go of any and all negative thoughts, especially related to the subject at hand.

This is important for any magical undertaking, but it's especially crucial when it comes to fertility, since your physical body is the literal location where the magic will manifest. Make sure that the energy you put into this work is coming from a relaxed, clear, and optimistic frame of mind.

You will need:

- 1 large green pillar candle
- Clary sage, ylang ylang, and/or geranium essential oil
- Symbol(s) of fertility
- Crystal point, athame, or other ritual carving tool

Instructions:

Carve your chosen fertility symbol into the candle. As you carve, visualize the joining of your life force with another to produce a new human being.

Anoint the candle with the oil, and then simply light the candle whenever you join with your mate.

Repeat the spell in the event that the candle has been spent before conception occurs.

SEVEN-DAY LUCK BOOSTING SPELL

Since ancient times, different cultures have held different beliefs about "luck." Many believed that the positions of the stars and planets ruled one's luck, while others petitioned creatures such as fairies and sprites to bring them luck. But whatever the merits of these traditions may be, it has been shown time and time again that approaching life with a positive attitude and a spirit of hopefulness has the most direct impact on our "luckiness" in life.

This fun spell harnesses the traditional color of luck while helping you to develop a more deliberate practice of positive thinking in your daily life.

You will need:

- 7 green votive candles
- 7 small slips of paper
- Green pencil, pen, or marker
- Small bowl

Instructions:

To prepare for this spell, write seven positive affirmations, one on each slip of paper. You can use the examples provided below, or write your own.

Fold each slip after writing the affirmation, and place them all in the bowl.

Place the seven candles in a row on your table or altar.

On the first morning of the spell, right after you wake up, light a single green candle. Swirl the pieces of paper around in the bowl and choose one at random. Read the affirmation out loud, and tuck one end of the slip of paper carefully under the lit candle. After a few moments, or when it's time to leave the house, gently extinguish the candle.

On the second morning, light the first candle again and a new candle, so that you have two green candles lit. Re-read the affirmation from the first morning, and then choose a new affirmation from the bowl to read aloud today. Tuck the new affirmation under the new candle, and leave both candles burning for a few moments or until it's time to leave the house.

Repeat this process for a full seven days. You will be delightfully surprised at how much "luck" you are tapping into as you increase your positive vibrations over the course of the week!

Example positive affirmations:

It is no accident that I am here on this Earth.
A million untold things work out for me every single day.
I am an excellent manifestor of my dreams.
Unexpected miracles happen every day.
I am lucky enough to have discovered magic.
I am really enjoying this experiment called "life."
I am wide open to the very best of possibilities.

BLUE

As the color of the sky on a sunny day, which we also see reflected in bodies of water, blue is a peaceful color with soothing properties, much like the effect of gazing at the ocean or a calmly flowing river. Accordingly, it is often used magically to bring about peace, calm, tranquility, and patience, helping us learn to "go with the flow" of life's unexpected twists and turns.

Blue is useful for sleep issues, including insomnia and disturbing dreams, and resolving anxiety in the mind and body. A truly healing color, blue can be used in magical workings to examine and resolve difficult emotions, and promote feelings of stability.

Blue is the color of the throat chakra, which governs deep communication and the ability to be honest with ourselves and others. Difficult conversations can be facilitated with spellwork involving this color, as blue helps us discover and speak our inner truths, and understand previously hidden truths about seemingly complex situations.

Its ability to help release stuck emotions makes it a great color for spellwork related to weight loss. It is also used in spellwork for protection from disharmony and negative vibrations, especially related to the home, and to promote wisdom, confidence, justice, and good fortune. Blue can assist with strengthening relationships of all kinds by promoting loyalty, sincerity, faith, devotion, reliability, and trust.

Blue is also associated with spiritual matters, and is used in workings related to psychic ability, astral projection, prophetic dreams, and meditation. If you are looking to increase your connection to the spiritual realm, be sure to work with the energies of blue. Blue's Elemental association is, of course, Water, and its cardinal direction is West. Astrologically, it is associated with the Moon, the planets Jupiter,

Neptune, and Mercury, and the signs of Virgo, Capricorn, Aquarius and Pisces.

Below, you'll find spellwork for protecting your home from negative energies and facilitating harmony among its inhabitants, increasing your capacity for patience, and becoming your own emotional guide and healer.

BLUE PERIMETER HOME PROTECTION SPELL

The vibrations of well-being that emanate from the color blue makes it an ideal color for a protection spell against negative energy—whether the negativity comes in the form of your own thoughts, other nonphysical energies within the home, or other people.

The subtle energetic adjustment created by this spell can help you turn your home into a true sanctuary, where the most positive and healing aspects of yourself and others can flourish.

This spell requires some extra caution, as you will be leaving lit candles temporarily unattended while you move from room to room. Make sure to take any necessary precautions regarding pets and children beforehand.

For best results, it's good to straighten up, sweep, dust, and/or whatever might be needed to create a sense of calm and order in the house. You may also want to purify the energy by smudging with herbs, or another space-clearing method.

<u>You will need:</u>

- Blue tea lights or votives (enough for each door and window into your home)
- Small bag or basket to carry candles

<u>Instructions:</u>

Place all of the candles in the bag or basket and hold it in your arms.

Focus on harnessing the energy of protection and concentrating it into all of the candles.

When you're ready, starting with the front entrance, place a blue candle on the floor at the center of the door. Light the candle, and visualize a blue wall of vibrant light sealing off this area of your home from unwanted energies and visitors.

Moving clockwise around your house, repeat these steps at every window and any additional doors—every potential entrance to your home. (If you have a working chimney, place one at the hearth as well.)

When you have reached the front entrance again, take a deep breath and visualize your entire home surrounded by protective blue light, and say the following (or similar) words:

"All energy within these walls is positive, peaceful, and for the good of all. And so it is."

Leave all the candles burning simultaneously for at least three minutes while you enjoy the feeling of security and peace permeating your living space.

To close the ritual, start again with the front entrance and gently extinguish the candle. Work clockwise again through the house, extinguishing each flame.

You can reuse these candles for atmosphere, or whenever you'd like to summon a feeling of reassurance while in your home.

HARMONY SPELL FOR DOMESTIC CONFLICTS

The Blue Perimeter Home Protection spell above is excellent for maintaining healthy and positive energy within your home. However, interpersonal conflicts among roommates or family members can still flare up and even persist over time. After all, we learn through our relationships, all of which are bound to have their thornier aspects at times.

This spell can facilitate that learning, and the resolution of the conflict, by providing a sacred space and time for honest and healing dialogue.

This spell is particularly effective because blue is the color of peace, and also because it requires that both parties be willing to work through and resolve a disagreement. (Note that it does require the willing physical participation of the other person involved.)

<u>You will need:</u>

- 1 blue pillar candle
- 2 pieces of blue or white yarn, long enough to wrap around the candle

<u>Instructions:</u>

You should sit facing one another with the candle placed between you, either at a table or on a raised platform, so that the candle is safe to handle once it's lit.

Take a moment to breathe and center yourself by visualizing a white light surrounding you both. Ask the other person to do the same, so that you both come to the ritual with healing intentions.

Light the candle and open an honest discussion about how to restore harmony in the home. Be frank, but respectful to one another. Practice using "I statements" (such as "I feel _____ when you _____" throughout the discussion.

It is important to avoid an attitude of blame or of right and wrong; rather, invite the person to work *with* you to solve the argument. This may take some time, so allow the space and time needed to truly clear the air and find resolution.

When you are each satisfied that you have been heard by the other and peace is restored, each person should carefully tie their piece of yarn around the candle to signify their commitment to keeping harmony in the home.

You can gently extinguish the candle at any point after this and relight it on each successive evening until the candle is spent.

SPELL FOR INCREASED PATIENCE

Whether you're experiencing frustrations at work, at home, within a relationship, or even simply with yourself, the healing properties of blue can assist you with releasing your pent-up negativity and harnessing patience in triggering situations.

This spell involves exploring your stress-based responses to the situation you need help with, and the creation of a talisman to help you move through future triggers with more grace and ease.

You will need:

- 1 blue spell candle
- Lavender, vetiver, palmarosa, and/or bergamot essential oil (optional)
- Journal or writing paper
- 1 blue adventurine, blue topaz, blue opal, or other blue mineral stone

Instructions:

Take a moment to relax and release the stress of the day. Breathe deeply and shift your focus from the world around you to the world inside you.

Anoint the candle with the oil, if using. Light the candle, and place the stone in front of it.

Begin freewriting about the relationship, job situation, family issue, etc. that has prompted you to work this spell.

Start by identifying the situation, and then write about how it makes you feel.

If you find yourself getting worked up about it as you write, try looking past your immediate reaction to what may be lying underneath the issue. Are there memories from your past trying to come up? Are there fears being activated by the current situation?

Write whatever comes to mind, and keep writing for at least 20 to 30 minutes.

When you feel clearer and more calm about the situation, take the blue stone and hold it between your palms. Visualize blue light radiating from within the stone and surrounding your entire body.

Hold this vision for a few moments, and when you're ready, say the following (or similar) words:

"Patience and peace,
ease and flow,
these old triggers I now let go.
So let it be."

Place the stone back in front of the candle and allow the candle to burn out on its own.

Carry the stone with you in your pocket or purse, and hold onto it whenever you experience a trigger that threatens your patience.

"LOVE NOTES TO SELF" MEDICINE SPELL

Encouragement and support from other people in our lives is a much-needed factor in healthy living. However, too much dependence on others creates imbalance, as we are ultimately each our own best friend, guide, and healer.

This spell is designed to provide you with the guidance and love of your higher self during times when you really need it, but might be less likely to be able to access these positive frequencies.

When worked with an appropriate amount of well-directed energy, this spell is incredibly powerful. This is because you're harnessing your most positive, peaceful, loving vibrations and storing them for when you need a lift out of more negative states like anxiety, despair, or just plain old energetic depletion.

Therefore, this is one of those workings that's best done well in advance of when you might actually benefit from it most. So the next time you find yourself on top of the world, take advantage of it and write yourself some magically charged "love notes"!

<u>You will need:</u>

- 1 blue candle
- Several small pieces of paper
- Blue pen, pencil, or marker
- Wax seal
- Small bowl

<u>Instructions:</u>

Take some time to quiet your mind, and then focus on the feelings of well-being that you are currently experiencing.

Light the candle, and begin to write yourself several positive "love notes" on the pieces of paper. Write as many as you can, with a minimum of at least seven.

For example, you might write "I love and appreciate who you are," or "I am so proud of all the work you have already done," or "You shine brightly, even when you don't know it!"

Fold each paper in thirds, overlapping so that the message is sealed inside.

By this point, the blue candle should have melted a good bit of wax. Drip a small amount of wax onto the fold of the paper and press the wax seal down to firmly secure it.

When the last note is sealed, gently extinguish the candle. Keep these notes in a small bowl on your table or altar. The next time you need some emotional TLC, take out a message from the bowl and read it! You may wish to keep the rest of the candle on hand for this purpose as well.

INDIGO

Associated with midnight skies and outer space, Indigo is perhaps the most mysterious color in the visible light spectrum. In fact, there has been much debate as to whether or not it actually even exists in what we think of as the rainbow.

Regardless, indigo is a color of intense spirituality, and is associated with the Akashic Records—the vast invisible realms where all information about every life ever lived can be accessed. As a blend of blue and violet, indigo contains properties of both colors, making it useful in magic related to healing, expression, spirituality, and esoteric insight.

Indigo is the color of the third eye, and helps bring forth inner knowledge from the subconscious. It is associated with the brow chakra (though violet plays this role in some systems), which governs perception, insight, clairvoyance, imagination, and dreams.

Use indigo's fluid energies for powerful results in workings related to psychic receptivity, intuition, and divination, as well as wisdom, sharpened perception, and discernment. Indigo facilitates deep meditative states, and guidance and healing on the spiritual level.

Indigo is also used in workings to aid with depression and improve focus, as well as balancing intense emotion with rational objectivity. It can be used to stop or counteract negative gossip and to slow down or halt an unwanted situation. In either of these cases, just be sure your focus is on the results you seek for yourself, rather than on manipulating others.

A color of dignity and self-mastery, indigo can help tame unwanted aspects of one's own character and support devotion to worthy people and causes in one's life. Indigo is associated with the planets Venus and Saturn, the signs of Gemini and Aquarius, and the Element of Air. Its cardinal direction is East.

The workings in this chapter utilize the special properties of indigo to help you get your own magical meditation practice going, increase your psychic receptivity, find clarity about a murky situation, and clear your physical body of unwanted energy.

INDIGO ZONE MEDITATION PRACTICE

It can be argued that all successful magic is worked in a meditative state—once the practitioner has successfully cleared their mind of all extraneous thoughts and concerns, making room for effective visualization of the magical goal. Yet many beginning Witches may struggle with this all-important step, since the mind pretty much always resists being quieted at first.

Getting into a regular meditation practice goes a long way toward boosting this aspect of your magic, and offers a range of physical, emotional, and mental benefits as well!

This ritual draws on the unique frequencies of indigo, and is designed to help you foster your own regular practice of getting in the "zone" for magic.

Be sure to make yourself as comfortable as you can—no need to sit cross-legged on the floor if that doesn't work for you. You can sit on pillows, in a chair, on the couch, etc. (You can even lie down, though if doing so will make you sleepy, then it's best to sit upright.)

You may also wish to play soft, simple music or other meditative sounds (such as Tibetan chimes) in the background. Try searching for free streaming ambient music online—you'll find plenty to choose from.

Just be sure that the sounds won't distract you—overly melodic or complex music tends not to be helpful. If you're in a place where noise is likely to interrupt you, try using earplugs for an easier time quieting your mind.

Finally, if you find that you need a more structured, guided mediation to get you in the flow, you can also find plenty of these online to listen to while the candle burns. Consider experimenting with a different guided meditation each day to see what works best for you.

You will need:

- 1 large indigo pillar candle
- Quiet, comfortable place to sit
- Timer
- Ambient/meditation music (optional)
- Earplugs (optional)

Instructions:

Light the candle and spend a few moments simply gazing softly at the flame. When you're ready to begin the meditation, set your timer for 5 minutes.

Now gently allow your eyes to close and take a slow, deep breath in through your nose.

Visualize the air flowing through your nose and down your throat, into your lungs. Then extend the breath into your heart center and down into your belly.

As you slowly release the breath, see it leaving your belly first, traveling back up through your heart center and your lungs, up through your throat and back out through your nose.

Repeat this breathing process three times.

Now allow yourself to breathe normally, keeping your attention on your inhale and exhale. When you find your mind wandering (and it almost certainly will), simply return your attention to your breath.

Be gentle and patient with your mind—you are asking it to do something it's unfamiliar with, and struggling or becoming frustrated will not help it quiet down.

Don't worry about how much or how often your mind wanders, since the mere act of trying to slow it down is benefiting you. Over time, with regular practice, meditation will become easier and more rewarding.

When the timer goes off, take a final deep, slow breath, gently open your eyes and extinguish the candle. You can reuse the candle for your subsequent meditations until it is spent.

Try this meditation for 5 minutes per day for three days, and then add a minute or two for the next three days. Gradually build up to at least 15 minutes per day, if you can.

Once you build this habit, getting into "the zone" for magic will be much easier!

INDIGO PSYCHIC RECEPTIVITY PRACTICE

This ritual can be used as a follow-up to the Indigo Zone Mediation Practice (above), or on its own. As a practice, it helps train the mind to enter a meditative state, but also opens you up specifically for messages from your subconscious to come through.

This is also a good "training" exercise for the Elemental Flame Communication exercise in the Violet chapter, below. Try it for a few days and see what kind of shifts occur in your awareness of the subtle energies within and outside of your mental space.

You will need:

- 1 indigo candle
- Small hand-held bell
- Journal or writing paper

Instructions:

Take a few deep, centering breaths to signal to your mind and body that it's time to turn inward, away from the distractions of the day.

Light the candle and ring the bell three times.

Let your gaze soften as you listen to the vibrations ripple ever outward, passing beyond your range of hearing and ultimately merging with all vibrations in the Universe.

As the sound of the bell fades, focus on the flame of the candle. Remain focused on the flame for as long as you can, but be sure to blink when you need to.

Whenever thoughts distract you from the flame, acknowledge them and then gently allow them leave your awareness. If you like, you can ring the bell again to recenter your focus. Stay in this meditative mode for at least 10 minutes.

Afterward, with the candle still burning, spend 10 to 15 minutes freewriting in your journal about anything that comes to mind.

You may write about thoughts that occurred to you during the mediation, any images you noticed in the candle flame, or simply whatever thoughts are flowing through your mind in the moment, however mundane they may seem.

After working this ritual a few times, reread your freewriting from each session and take note of any patterns that come up.

SPELL FOR CLARITY

Our analytical minds often don't want to leave a problem alone, even when we know we can't figure out a solution just yet. This can actually keep the problem around longer than it needs to be, as we keep it active in our vibrational frequencies through our thoughts about it. In these instances, clarity cannot arise until we have let go of the problem completely, at least for a moment.

This is a great spell for moving toward resolution of any kind of "muddy" situation—a decision to make, a seemingly intractable problem, or a vague sense of something being wrong that you can't quite identify. Rather than over-thinking and over-analyzing the question, you will be allowing your inner knowing to bring clarity to the situation. Indigo helps connect us to the etheric plane through our Third Eye (or pineal gland), bypassing the analytical mind to receive pure wisdom.

This spell can be worked on its own or in conjunction with the Indigo Zone Meditation Practice, above. (For best results, use a new indigo candle, in addition to your meditation candle, for this working.) You may also wish to use earplugs and/or ambient music to help you keep your focus.

You will need:

- 1 indigo tea light, votive, or spell candle
- Timer (optional)
- Journal or writing paper (optional)

Instructions:

To begin, identify your question or issue, and state it out loud as you light the candle. If you like, you can say the following (or similar) words:

"From my subconscious mind, connected to All That Is, I call forth clarity on __________."

Spend a few moments simply gazing softly at the flame and breathing deeply. When you feel ready, close your eyes and touch the index and middle fingers of your dominant hand to the center of your forehead, just above your brows. This is the opening to your third eye, where your access to intuition and psychic visions resides.

Visualize the light of the candle floating into your conscious awareness, behind your closed eyelids. Hold this vision as long as possible, and simply relax into this meditative state. (If you like, set a timer at the start of the spell for at least 7 minutes.)

Don't think about your question—surrender it instead to the subconscious. If you find yourself getting distracted, gently return your focus to the flame at your third eye.

When you are finished, you can write down any messages or impressions that came to you during the ritual. However, don't expect the answer to your question to come right away—it may need to percolate in your subconscious for awhile until the time is right for you to receive the information.

Just go on about your day, and if your attention gets stuck back on the issue, remind yourself that it is being resolved behind the scenes, and that you will know what to do when the time is right.

SPIRITUAL CLEANSING BATH

If you've been feeling tired, stressed, anxious, or depressed with no obvious cause, it may be time to clear your body of old or unwanted energies.

The power of natural Himalayan salts is well-known for its detoxifying properties—not just on the physical level, but on the spiritual level as well. The energetic vibrations of indigo enhance the work by helping you achieve and maintain a calm, meditative state.

Note: if you have not worked with Himalayan salts before, it's advisable to start with a smaller amount, as its detoxifying effects can cause drowsiness or dizziness. Keep a glass of water to drink near the tub in case you begin to feel weak or sleepy.

<u>You will need:</u>

- 4 indigo candles
- ½ to 1 cup fine-grain Himalayan salt
- Bergamot, lavender, patchouli, and/or vetiver essential oils (optional)
- Drinking water (optional)

<u>Instructions:</u>

Begin by placing an indigo candle at each corner of your bathtub.

Run the water at a comfortable temperature.

Once the bottom of the tub is covered in water, pour in the salt. When the tub is full, light each of the candles with healing and clearing intentions.

Gently submerge yourself in the water and shed all of the stress of the day through focusing on your breathing. Allow your mind to clear.

When you are ready, visualize the light of the four candles uniting above you and entering your cleansed body to heal and refresh your spirit.

Stay in the tub for at least 20 minutes and up to 45 minutes.

When you are done, drain the bathtub and exit carefully. Gently extinguish the candles, and treat yourself to a relaxing evening as your body integrates the effects of the ritual bath.

VIOLET

A color found in delicate flowers as well as spectacular sunrises and sunsets, violet is the highest vibration of the colors in the visible spectrum. It contains the energies of both red and blue, with characteristics of each to be found in its magical purview.

The influence of red makes this color appropriate for workings related to power, success, and ambition, as well as increased enthusiasm for an endeavor. The blue aspects are excellent for magic connected with spirituality, wisdom, emotional healing and attaining hidden knowledge. Violet is also commonly referred to as "purple," and while there are technically distinctions between these two colors, they can be thought of as one and the same for the purposes of candle magic.

Those who work with the color indigo will notice a fair amount of overlap with violet when it comes to magical purposes, but there are some important distinctions. Where indigo's powers are primarily concerned with inner mysteries, violet is more about tuning into broader, universal energies.

Violet is associated with the crown chakra (although in some systems, the color white plays this role), which governs connections to the universal higher consciousness. As such, violet is used in workings related to spiritual development and connecting to one's higher self, as well as developing and strengthening psychic ability. All aspects of occult wisdom are applicable here, including divination, meditation, magic, astral travel, dream recall, and other forms of mysticism.

As a color of spiritual healing and development, violet is used in workings related to psychic protection and restoring balance to empaths and other energetically sensitive people. Violet also promotes nurturing qualities, humility, forgiveness, and devotion to a person or a cause. In some traditions, violet is used to bring an end to bad luck. Violet is associated with the Element of Air, the planets Mercury, Saturn, and Jupiter, and the signs of Capricorn, Gemini, and Sagittarius. Its cardinal direction is East.

In this chapter, you'll find spells and rituals for communicating with the higher realms through the Element of Fire, increasing your capacity for joy, strengthening your devotion to an activity or cause, and transmuting negativity through spiritual alchemy.

ELEMENTAL FLAME COMMUNICATION

This exercise builds and strengthens your "psychic muscles" by directly interacting with the flame of your candle. You are actively connecting with the higher realms of consciousness—the domain of the color violet—in the form of the Element of Fire.

Note: For optimal results, you may want to spend a few days with the Indigo Zone Meditation Practice and/or the Indigo Psychic Receptivity Practice (above) before trying this one.

You will need:

- 1 violet pillar candle
- Journal or writing paper (optional)

Instructions:

Spend a few moments quieting your mind. When you are ready to begin, light the candle as you invoke the Element of Fire with the following (or similar) words:

"Element of Fire, thank you for the warmth and light you provide for all on Earth. I welcome your presence and your communication in this timeless moment. Blessed Be."

Gently train your gaze on the flame of the candle (be sure to blink when you need to).

Begin by simply watching the flame and taking mental note of its appearance. Is it still, or is it flickering rapidly? Is the flame rising high or leaning in any particular direction? Every candle is different, and every candle flame is a unique energetic presence in the Universe. Get acquainted with the spirit of this flame for a moment or two.

When you feel ready, begin trying to "shape" the flame with your own visualization of its appearance. With your eyes still open and trained on the flame, visualize it growing, shrinking, getting brighter and dimmer, leaning in a particular direction, flickering, waving, etc.

Keep your focus trained on the flame and the change you're visualizing at the same time. See how in-sync you can get the actual flame to be with your projection. You will have more success with this over time, with regular practice.

Finally, let go of working to shape the flame, and simply observe it again. Let your focus go very soft, and watch for images taking shape within the flame.

What do you see? What impressions or messages seem to be coming through? Spend a few moments in this receptive mode, without trying to analyze what you see.

When you feel finished, with the candle still burning, try spending 10 to 15 minutes freewriting in your journal about your experience. How did the flame respond to your visualizations of its size, direction, etc.? What images or other sensory data came through during the exercise?

After working this ritual a few times, reread your freewriting from each session and take note of any patterns that come up.

JOYFUL CROWN CHAKRA CONNECTION SPELL

This spell is designed to help you connect with the higher vibrational frequencies that allow you to attract more joy into your life. You are taking the feelings of joy that you experience in your heart center and pulling them up through your chakra system into the crown, where you can then experience a deeper connection with Universal higher consciousness. For it is in the deep feeling of joy that we know we are where we are meant to be!

Displaying the lists of joyful elements in your life helps to seal the energetic benefits of the spell. You may wish to keep them on your altar, place them on a vision board, or leave them somewhere else where you will see them often.

You will need:

- 3 violet candles
- 3 pieces of paper
- Violet marker or pen

Instructions:

On your altar or workspace, set up the three candles and place one piece of paper in front of each. Spend some time quieting your mind.

When you feel ready, light the first candle. Now take the paper in front of it and write down the names of all of the people that bring joy into your life. (You can use both sides of the paper if need be!)

Light the second candle and write down all of the places that make you feel joyful. These can be as simple as a sunny window in your home or as grand as the ocean.

Light the third candle and write down all of the experiences that bring joy into your life. These can be memories, but should also include recurring experiences that you still have access to.

If you wish, you can use additional sheets of paper to freewrite in more detail about these experiences, or you can just jot them down in note form.

When you are finished writing, gather all three of your lists and read them aloud, taking turns among the three categories. For example, read a name or two from the first list, and then read a place or two, then an experience.

Once you have read aloud all of the items on all three lists, hold the papers in your hands and say the following (or similar) words of gratitude:

"My life is filled with wonderful people, beautiful places, and joyful experiences. Blessed Be."

Place the lists somewhere where they will be frequently visible to you.

You can leave the candles burning, or gently extinguish them and relight them when you want to summon up a feeling of joyful connection to the Universe.

DEVOTION REVITALIZATION SPELL

Most of us have had the experience of starting a new hobby or activity—such as learning to play an instrument, studying a foreign language, or joining a book club—only to find that a few weeks or months later, our enthusiasm for the activity or cause has waned. This is often accompanied by at least some level of guilt or self-shaming for not "sticking it out," which is never helpful!

The next time you find your momentum flagging around an extracurricular that you do actually enjoy, try this spell instead of getting down on yourself for losing steam. Devotion can be cultivated and revitalized with some simple energetic adjustments—as long as you truly desire it!

<u>You will need:</u>

- 1 violet pillar candle
- Lemon, cedarwood, cinnamon, and/or patchouli essential oil
- Work candle for atmosphere
- Crystal point, athame, or other ritual carving tool
- Journal or writing paper (optional)

<u>Instructions:</u>

Light the work candle and spend some time quieting your mind.

Find a symbol that represents the activity or cause you're focusing on. You can use something emblematic of the activity (a soccer ball, a book, etc.) or an abstract symbol, such as a rune or a pentacle, that represents the devotion you're seeking to revitalize. Carve this symbol into the front of the violet candle, and anoint the candle with the oil.

Spend a few moments visualizing the feeling you had when you first began engaging with this activity. Enjoy the sensation of the excitement, ambition, anticipation, etc. that drove you to move from just thinking about the activity to actually doing it.

Now, focus on what you still truly enjoy about the activity. Make a list, either on paper or mentally, of every detail about it that makes the pursuit of it worthwhile. (If you feel any negativity creeping into your thoughts, such as notions of failure or guilt, etc., let them go and return your focus to the positive aspects.)

Finally, visualize a goal you can work toward, such as a particular level of skill/ability in the activity, that will enhance your enjoyment of it.

When you've reached a place of feeling enthusiasm again and are ready to seal this energy, light the candle as you say the following (or similar) words:

"I celebrate the joy that [name of activity] brings
and rekindle my devotion to that joy.
Blessed Be."

Allow the candle to burn for at least several more minutes before gently extinguishing it. Whenever you'd like to quickly rejuvenate your passion for the activity again, relight the candle and recall your visualizations from the spell.

VIOLET FLAME TRANSMUTATION RITUAL

This spell borrows from the ancient teachings of the Violet Flame, an alchemical energy known to many different spiritual traditions. Through this visualization, you can call on the Violet Flame for assistance with any kind of change you wish to manifest in your life.

Here, the focus is on transmuting the negative energy of unwanted memories. If you find yourself dogged by thoughts or reminders of an old experience that triggers sadness, anger, regret, or shame, bring in the healing power of the Violet Flame to set you free from those energetic attachments and create positive new experiences in their place.

Be sure to spend some time in meditation, or another form of grounding and centering, before this ritual, and work in a quiet and comfortable place where you will not be disturbed.

You will need:

- 1 violet spell or taper candle
- Work candle for atmosphere (optional)

Instructions:

Light the work candle, if using. Light the violet candle and focus your attention on the flame for a few moments.

When you're ready, close your eyes, bring the flame into your mind's eye, and say the following (or similar) words:

"I ask the Universal presence of the Violet Flame to manifest within me now."

With your eyes still closed, see the bright fiery color of the candle flame turning into a luminescent violet, and watch as the violet flame grows to fill your entire body.

When your body is fully alight with the flame, spin the flame in a clockwise direction throughout your physical form.

Now state your intention for transmuting the unwanted, with the following (or similar) words:

"I transmute the energies of these memories that no longer serve me. They are consumed in the Violet Flame."

Now it's time to state your intentions for what the transmuted energy can become, with the following (or similar) words:

"I am now filled with the energies of happiness and joy, and free to make new memories."

Take a deep breath, and when you're ready, slowly open your eyes. Take a moment to acknowledge the transmutation that has taken place, and the spiritual presence that assisted you. You can simply say something like:

"Thanks be to the Violet Flame for this change."

You can leave the candle burning, or gently extinguish it to use again for another Violet Flame ritual.

WHITE

As the sum total of all colors in the spectrum of visible light, white has long been associated with the qualities of unity, wholeness, truth, and peace. White represents the highest level of consciousness available to living beings. It symbolizes the "blank slate," the point of infinite potentiality for new creation within every moment. Perhaps this is why a white candle can be used in substitution for any other color when used in candle magic.

As a highly spiritual color, white is used in magical workings related to enlightenment, initiations, connecting to one's higher self, accessing the Akashic records, and other paths to spiritual growth. It is often associated with the crown chakra, which governs connection to the universal higher consciousness (although in some systems, violet plays this role).

White's purifying energies are used for cleansing and consecrating ritual tools and spaces, but can also be used to clear up confusion around complex situations. White is also used in magic related to inspiration and healing, new beginnings, completions, and balance, especially of one's personal energy.

White brings clarity to the cluttered mind, and aids with social anxiety, helping people to feel more comfortable and even extroverted around others. It is also associated with safety, making it great for protection workings. Its peaceful, unity-promoting properties make it ideal for workings related to conflict resolution, whether between individuals or groups of people, and for fresh starts after arguments or other troubles.

White has feminine energy and is often used to represent the Goddess in ritual. It is associated with the Moon and the sign of Pisces, as well as the Element of Air, making East its cardinal direction.

However, white is also the color of the Fifth Element, also known as Akasha or Spirit. In this sense, white has no cardinal direction, but is instead associated with all directions.

You can use a white candle in place of any other candle in any spell in this book. This can be very handy when you have a particular magical need but no time to go out and buy the color that the spell calls for.

For an extra magical boost in this scenario, try also including crystals, ribbons, an altar cloth, or other objects that do visually represent the color you're actually working with. For example, if using a white candle in place of violet, add an amethyst or two to your altar or work space for the duration of the spell.

In this chapter, you'll find spells to bring clarity and new perspective to a situation, purify ritual and magical tools, work for peace in the world, and strengthen your physical body with the energy of white light.

"SPINNING WHEELS" CLARITY SPELL

When you're dealing with a problem that seems to refuse all possible solutions, it can be easy to keep spinning the same thoughts about it over and over in your mind. The fact is, you'll never come to a solution when you're still focused on the problem—you have to remove yourself from the vibrational frequency of the problem first.

This is easier said than done, of course, but with a sufficiently open mind, the following spell can get you there. The combination of white candle magic, quartz crystals, and the willingness to allow your subconscious mind to create new pathways to understanding the problem will help you get out of the "mud" in your mind and into a space where you can see things clearly again. This spell is ideally worked at night, shortly before going to bed.

You will need:

- 1 white pillar or taper candle
- 3 or more small quartz crystals
- Vetiver, peppermint, or clary sage essential oil
- Journal or writing paper

Instructions:

Anoint the candle with the oil. Place the quartz crystals around the candle in a circle (if using three stones, create a triangle, with one of the points nearest you). Take a few moments to quiet your mind.

When you're ready, light the candle, and begin to write.

You can start by identifying the problem, and then freewrite about how you're feeling about it at this moment.

Then write about how you will feel when the problem is solved—not how you will solve it, but simply what it will feel like when this particular problem is behind you.

Continue to write whatever comes to mind, without trying to direct yourself to a solution.

You may soon find yourself changing the subject altogether—if so, go with it! You are allowing your subconscious mind to merge with the vibrational frequencies of the candle and the quartz.

Continue to freewrite for at least 15 minutes, if not longer, until you feel a peaceful sense of detachment from the original topic.

When you're finished, gently extinguish the candle. Place one of the quartz crystals under your pillow before going to sleep, and pay attention to anything your dreams have to tell you.

Depending on your circumstances, you may wish to repeat the spell another time or two until you have the clarity you need to find your solution.

MAGICAL TOOLS CLEANSING RITUAL

Here's a simple, effective method for clearing out old energy from tools you use regularly in ritual and magic, such as your wand, athame, chalice, magical jewelry, talismans or charms (provided they're fire-proof!).

You may wish to clear your tools once a year, or more often, depending on your personal practice.

<u>You will need:</u>

- 3 white taper or pillar candles
- Copal or sandalwood incense
- Ritual/magical tools to be cleansed

<u>Instructions:</u>

Line the candles up in a horizontal row, a few inches apart, on your altar or work space. Light the incense and the candles. Take a moment to quiet your mind.

When you're ready to begin, pick up the item you wish to cleanse. Pass it quickly through the flame of each candle, visualizing all unwanted energy being "burned up" in the fire of each flame.

Repeat this with each ritual/magical item that needs to be cleared. When you have finished, gently extinguish the candles. You can reuse the candles for another cleansing ritual in the future, or use them for atmosphere in other workings.

GLOBAL PEACE SPELL

The goal of world peace is a noble one indeed, but clearly this is beyond the powers of any individual Witch, or it would have been accomplished by now! Nonetheless, we know that collective energy focused in a specific way can create amazing changes.

If you wish, you can contribute *very* powerful personal energy toward the collective goal of universal peace. This delightful spell provides an avenue for you to send strength and light to people all around the world.

<u>You will need:</u>

- 1 white spell candle
- Map of the world

<u>Instructions:</u>

Take a few deep breaths, releasing any negative thoughts on each exhale. When you're ready, light the candle.

As you allow some of the wax to melt, summon the feeling of peace within yourself. How does it feel when all is well in your world, with no conflicts disturbing your circle of family and friends? Imagine this feeling extending from you and radiating out in all directions, until it covers the entire planet.

Once a fair amount of wax has melted, begin working with your map.

First, send white light to the entire Earth, both the land and the oceans, until the map is bathed in white light in your mind's eye.

Now, working with one continent at a time, visualize the people living in each area of the world, and imagine sending the white light of peace to them.

Place a drop of wax on each continent to seal in your well wishes for peace in that area. As you do so, say the following (or similar) words:

"Peace begins within
and flows outward in infinite waves.
I send peace to all who dwell here,
as they and I are One.
Blessed Be."

When you have finished, take a final deep breath and gently extinguish the candle. Place the map on your altar or bury it in the Earth to send peace throughout.

WHITE LIGHT HEALING SPELL

While modern medicine has indeed made unprecedented progress in helping us heal from severe accidents and illnesses of all sorts, today's doctors are still largely unaware of the powers of the mind-body connection when it comes to our own ability to heal ourselves.

This spell is not meant to replace needed medical care, but it can work wonders in helping the body restore itself to its natural state of well-being. Whether you're dealing with a minor illness or injury or a serious medical condition, try working with healing white light in conjunction with your current treatment. Never underestimate the power of your own personal energy to improve your health!

Meditative music adds an extra healing effect to this spell. If you don't have any recordings of soothing music or nature sounds, search for free streaming ambient music online—you'll find plenty to choose from.

<u>You will need:</u>

- 9 white tea lights or votive candles
- Ambient music (optional)

<u>Instructions:</u>

Turn on the meditation music, if desired.

Sit on the floor or in a chair in the center of the room. Place the candles around you in a circle and then take several deep breaths, focusing on each inhale and exhale, to quiet your mind and focus your attention on your body.

When you're ready, light the candles one at a time, beginning in the cardinal direction of East and moving in a clockwise direction.

Once all nine candles are lit, sit back in the middle of the circle.

Close your eyes and focus your attention back on your breath for three counts.

Visualize a white light beginning in your heart center and gently spreading throughout your body. See the light pulsing into each area of your body, one at a time—your core, your legs and feet, shoulders, arms, hands, throat, and crown of the head.

Now focus extra white light in the area of your body you are working to heal.

Continue to breathe deeply, and envision all unwanted energy flowing out and away from your body as the white light continues to pulse through you. Maintain this visualization, breathing deeply, for at least 15 minutes.

When you are finished, gently extinguish the candles. Repeat the ritual daily, using the same candles, until the candles are spent. Depending on your body's needs, you may want to continue this practice for an extended period of time.

BLACK

As the counterpart to white, the sum of all colors, black is the result of the absence of light, and is therefore technically the absence of color. However, we still experience the color black in the night sky, in materials deep within the earth, and in many plant and animal species.

It's fair to say that black has had a negative reputation over the centuries, often associated with unpleasant topics like death and evil. In the realm of magic, black has definitely been associated with harmful or manipulative workings. However, those who work in accordance with the tenet of "do no harm" know how to utilize the energies of black for a variety of positive purposes.

Black is widely used in protection magic, as its ability to repel negative energy is unparalleled on the color wheel. (Many people who wear a lot of black clothing are sensitive, empathic types who are actually shielding themselves from the energies of others, whether or not they realize it.)

Black candles can be used in workings related to deflecting psychic attack, undoing negative workings, and banishing and/or binding negative influences. However, if you're dealing with other people in an emotionally charged situation, you may want to first consider other magical solutions, as black can be incredibly powerful in this context and may bring unintended consequences.

Black is excellent for increasing or reinforcing personal power (which, along with its protective properties, may be why Witches like to wear it so much!) and promoting independence. It is also the color of endings and release, making it ideal for workings related to ending unwanted habits, marking the end of a particular phase in life, dissolving obstacles, and getting out of relationships, jobs, or other unwanted circumstances.

It aids with transitions and transformations, lending stability to help one stay grounded and focused in the midst of upheaval. A color of hidden knowledge, black is useful for workings related to both keeping and discovering secrets, as well as divination techniques such as scrying or reading tea leaves.

Black is associated with the planet Saturn as well as the dark phase of the Moon. Its Elemental associations are Air and Earth, and its cardinal directions are East and North.

In the spells below, you'll work with black to banish negativity from yourself and from your home, shield yourself from external negativity, and activate a personal transformation.

CRYSTALLINE PROTECTION SHIELD

As you travel through your day, you encounter a multitude of energies—from other people, from situations, even from the vibrational echoes of events that occurred in a specific place. Much of this energy is positive, or at least neutral, but negative energy can be an unnecessary obstacle to feeling the way you want to feel.

The shielding qualities of black, combined with the talismanic properties of protective crystals, come together in this spell to help you create a vibrational shield of protection from any unwanted energies you may come across. This spell is particularly excellent for empaths, but is also useful for anyone who deals with a lot of different people and/or places in their daily life.

You will need:

- 1 black candle
- Cinnamon, clove, juniper, vetiver, or ylang ylang essential oil

- 1 piece of jade, jet, black tourmaline, or other protective crystal

Instructions:

Take a moment to breathe, relax, and release any stress you are feeling.

When you are ready, anoint the candle with the oil, light it, and place it in front of you. Pick up the protective crystal and hold it between your palms.

Now close your eyes and visualize the light emanating from the candle creating a protective shield around you.

See it start small and grow larger to encompass your entire body. Feel the light making a shield around you to protect you from any external negativity or ill will. Hold the light shield in your mind and strengthen its powers.

When you are ready, open your eyes, gently extinguish the candle, and know that you have created your own personal protection layer of light and love to carry with you through your daily life.

Carry the crystal with you in your pocket or purse as an added reminder to "activate" the protective shield.

You can repeat this spell any time you feel you need a renewed boost of protection against any unwanted energetic influences.

PERSONAL NEGATIVITY BANISHING SPELL

The first spell in this chapter is about protection from external negative energy—that which comes from influences outside of ourselves. When it comes to our *own* personal negative energy (and we all have some, at one point or another!), then a different approach is needed.

Magically, black is the color of banishing. A banishing, being the opposite of a summoning, is used to utterly un-invite something from your life. No life is completely without difficulty, and when something unwanted happens to us, a bit of negative energy from the experience often stays with us. This negative energy build-up can be seen as layers of dust upon our psyche.

This spell is a powerful banishing you can use as often as needed to give your spirit a good dusting off, and clear the way to healing, less stress, and the ability to truly move past difficulties.

<u>You will need:</u>

- 1 black candle
- 1 work candle for atmosphere
- Small slips of paper
- Fire-proof dish
- Journal or writing paper (optional)

<u>Instructions:</u>

Light the atmosphere candle and take a few moments to ground and center yourself.

When you're ready, begin writing in your journal about whatever it is that has caused you to want to work this spell, whether it's a current problem, an old memory, a feeling of generalized anxiety, etc.

As you write, know that you are emptying the negative energy from your physical body onto the page.

When you feel you have written enough, choose a few words or phrases that encapsulate the negative topics you have just written about. Write these on the small slips of paper. (You may only need one slip of paper for this, or you may want several—this is entirely up to you.)

Now light the black candle.

Take the first slip of paper and hold it over the candle flame until it ignites, then drop it into the dish to continue burning out on its own.

As you do so, say, *"I fully release the energy of__________."* Repeat this process for the remaining slips of paper.

When you are done, gently extinguish the candle.

For the next few days, you may wish to note any significant dreams or shifts in energy that occur and write them down in your journal.

FIRE-AND-WATER HOUSE CLEANSING SPELL

The Blue Perimeter Home Protection spell, above, is great for keeping negative energy from entering your home. This spell, on the other hand, works to expel negative energy from *within* your dwelling space, and is quite handy for those living in old buildings.

This is an excellent spell to try when no amount of smudging (with sage, sweetgrass, or other powerful herbs) seems to quite get rid of all the less-than-pleasant energies in your home.

For best results, sweep or vacuum each room in the house before you begin, and close all windows.

You will need:

- 1 black floating candle
- Small bucket or cauldron

Instructions:

Fill the bucket or cauldron with water. Light the candle and float it on the surface of the water.

Beginning with the room(s) furthest from your front door, stand in the center of each room in your home.

Close your eyes and visualize all of the negative energy in the room being drawn to the flame of the candle. As it nears the cauldron or bucket, the energy is diverted by the flame into the water, where it is neutralized.

Once all of the negative energy has been drawn into the water, move to the next room, making your way toward the front door one room at a time.

When you are finished, stand near the front door and gently extinguish the candle.

Open the door and carry the bucket or cauldron outside. Take it all the way out to the street you live on (or the edge of your property), remove the candle, and pour the water out onto the Earth. Discard the candle in an outdoor trash can.

When you return to your home, open at least one window in each room, leaving it open for at least five minutes.

If you like, burn some sweetgrass or palo santo to enhance the energetic shifts now taking place.

TRANSFORMATION TALISMAN

Just as it takes an immense amount of pressure for the sand inside an oyster to transform into a pearl, personal transformation can be a slow and intense process. But, as any practitioner of magic learns, personal transformation is essential to a continually fulfilling life.

Whether you're working to lose weight, release an unwanted habit, regain independence after a breakup, or manifest any other daunting transformation, this spell will help you focus your positive intentions into a physical representation symbolizing this change. Enjoy the process of this spell, and then enjoy the enlivening process of transformation!

The shape of your talisman is up to you, but it should be fairly simple and represent the transformation you intend to achieve. Runes and other magical symbols can work well here, but you may also intuit your own original design. Just be aware that the more complex the symbol, the less sturdy it will be as a finished object.

You will need:

- 1 black taper candle
- Sand
- Bowl
- Journal or writing paper (optional)
- Small cloth bag (optional)

Instructions:

Place the sand in a bowl on your altar or table. Take a moment to relax and center yourself in your space.

Light the candle and set your intent of transformation. Spend some time conjuring up the feeling you want to have when you have accomplished your goal.

When you have a solid hold on this vision, draw your chosen symbol neatly in the sand, using your index finger.

When enough of the wax has melted, pour it into the design in the sand. You may have to allow extra time for more wax to melt to fill your shape. If so, continue to focus on your desired outcome. You may wish to journal about your goal during this time.

When you have filled the symbol with wax, place the bowl in the refrigerator or freezer for the wax to harden.

Once it has become solid, pop the wax shape out and clean any extra sand off of it.

Hold it in your hands and focus again on your transformational goal, and gently extinguish the candle.

You can keep your talisman on your altar to remind you of your goal, or carry it in a small cloth bag with you in your pocket, backpack, or purse.

SILVER

The feminine energy and enigmatic quality of the color silver has long linked it with the energy of the Moon, which is often said to cast a silvery light. Named for the precious metal that also bears this color, silver is a powerful, mysterious hue associated with all things psychic and divine.

As such, silver is often used in magical workings related to psychic awareness, whether it's clairvoyance, clairaudience, other forms of telepathy, or mediumship. Silver is good for strengthening intuition and divination skills and enhancing meditation, dream recall, and astral travel.

It is a color associated with wisdom and feminine power, and helps strengthen one's connection with the energies of the divine realms. It's also good for spellwork related to female fertility.

Silver's reflective properties can be used to help see into one's true self, which can help with navigating difficult or complex situations. It can also help with the frustrations often experienced when dealing with life's mysteries, by promoting patience and calm in the face of the unknown.

As a color with very fluid energies, silver helps one get better at "going with the flow" in quickly changing circumstances, and its similarity to the color grey makes it good for workings related to maintaining neutrality.

Silver is also used in spellwork for victory in endeavors involving luck, such as gambling, and is known to aid in attracting money quickly. It is a good color for workings related to intelligence and memory, particularly when thinking quickly is required, as well as stability, communication, and finding lost items.

Silver is a primary color of the Goddess and is used to represent her in Wiccan ritual, as well as for invoking or "drawing down" the Moon at Esbats. It is also associated with the signs of Gemini and Cancer, and the Element of Water. Its cardinal direction is West.

The spells in this chapter work with the energies of silver to reconnect with the divine feminine, connect psychically with the Element of Water, increase your gambling luck, and find lost items.

SILVER GODDESS-RECONNECTION SPELL

This spell is ideal for anyone who feels they have drifted from their spiritual path (which we all do from time to time). It's a lovely way to renew, to realign, and to reconnect with your personal relationship to the higher realms. It's a great spell for Wiccans in particular, but you don't actually have to worship the Goddess, or any goddess at all, to experience a deeper resonance with your own spiritual source.

Ultimately, this is about tapping into the essence of the divine feminine, which we all are a part of, no matter our individual beliefs. In the hustle and bustle of daily life, many of us are primarily engaged with masculine, or "yang" energy—the energy of "doing." Coming into greater balance means working with feminine, or "yin" energy as well, and learning to embrace "being."

You will be creating a magical talisman from a piece of jewelry with the vibrational frequencies of silver. You can use a favorite piece of silver jewelry or purchase a new one for this working. (Note: the jewelry doesn't have to be made of actual silver—a silver-colored piece will work fine.)

For an extra boost of the divine feminine energy, try this working on a New Moon or a Full Moon.

You will need:

- 3 silver spell candles

- 1 work candle for atmosphere (preferably white)
- Your favorite anointing oil (a single oil or a blend)
- Piece of silver jewelry

Instructions:

Light the work candle and arrange the three candles in a triangle on your altar or workspace. The base of the triangle should be facing you.

Anoint the jewelry with the oil, while focusing your intention on reconnecting with the divine feminine. Place the anointed jewelry in the center of the triangle.

Light the left base candle and say the following (or similar) words: *"I greet you, Goddess, at this new starting point along my path."*

Light the candle at the top of the triangle and say the following (or similar) words: *"I greet you, Mother Earth, every day that I walk upon you."*

Light the right base candle and say the following (or similar) words: *"I greet you, divine feminine, on all the days of my journey."*

To close the ritual, say the following (or similar) words:

"I thank you, Goddess, Mother Earth, divine feminine, for this time and place, this reconnection, and your eternal presence. Blessed Be."

Allow the candles to burn out on their own.

Wear the jewelry for ritual and magic, and/or in your everyday life.

TEMPERANCE WATER RITUAL

This soothing, meditative ritual is great for mulling over complicated issues, helping you to have the patience to allow things to work out in their own perfect timing. It's also great for simply calming the nerves, tapping into your psychic powers, and even getting into an ideal magical headspace prior to Esbats or any other ritual celebrations.

Here, you will be physically embodying the symbolism of the Temperance card, the 14th Major Arcana card of the Tarot. Virtually all Tarot decks feature the same basic image on this card: a figure, often female, who is pouring water back and forth between two vessels.

The symbolism is that of communication between the worlds, as well as of the need for balance and patience. The feminine energies and watery symbolism of the card makes it a perfect partner to the fluid vibrational frequencies of silver, combining in a ritual that promotes patience and calm, and welcomes psychic impressions, divine messages, and intuitive, non-verbal communication between your higher self and your subconscious mind.

If you don't have a Tarot deck, you can print an image of the Temperance card from any number of websites (or if you're artistically inclined, you can draw your own!). As for the dish ware, these items can be black, white, or silver colored (stainless steel is perfect).

<u>You will need:</u>

- 2 silver taper candles
- Large bowl or basin
- 2 cups
- Pitcher of water
- Temperance Tarot card (or image)
- Journal or writing paper (optional)

<u>Instructions:</u>

Place the bowl or basin between the two silver candles. Place the Temperance card where you can see it, but not so close to the water as to risk getting wet.

Light the candles and then pour the water very slowly from the pitcher into the bowl. If you like, speak some words about whatever dilemma (if any) you're working the spell in relation to, and ask for any advice or insight that may be available now.

Holding one cup in each hand, scoop and pour water from one cup to the other. Do this a few times, and then empty both cups back into the bowl and start again.

Continue to play with the water in this fashion as you feel yourself relaxing and your mind quieting.

Observe the water as it swirls around in the bowl, noting tiny details of bubbles, splashes and whirls as well as how the light bounces off of the water.

Allow any thoughts that come into the forefront to be noted and released, but don't try to "solve" anything—just softly play with the water. You may wish from time to time to gaze at the Temperance card, and see if any messages come through the imagery.

Continue to work with the water for at least 5 minutes, or until you feel a sense of serenity and completion take hold. If you wish, write down any thoughts or impressions related to the issue you spoke about when you first poured the water.

When you're finished with the ritual, gently extinguish the candles and pour the water outside on a tree or in the grass.

LUCKY-COIN GAMBLING SPELL

For those who enjoy the occasional trip to the casino or friendly poker game, here's a spell for a talisman to bring silver's lucky energy along.

Keep it hidden and secret, lest you allow any doubt to be introduced into your vibration. Good luck!

<u>You will need:</u>

- 1 silver spell candle
- Patchouli or cinnamon essential oil (optional)
- A silver coin (ideally a collector's item or foreign currency or something else you wouldn't spend)

<u>Instructions:</u>

Anoint the candle with the oil, if using. (You might also wish to anoint the coin.)

Place the coin in front of the candle.

Light the candle and as you allow some of the wax to melt, visualize having success at gambling.

Whether it's a card game, a slot machine, or any other game of chance, summon up the feeling of winning. See and feel the prize money in your hands.

Be as detailed with your visualization as possible, and stay focused on the vibrational frequency of the delight in winning.

When enough wax has melted, carefully tilt the candle to drip a drop of wax onto the "heads" side of the coin.

Replace the candle, and hold the coin several inches above the flame as you say the following (or similar) words:

"Lucky silver, lucky coin,
bring me luck and bring me gain.
Lucky money, lucky life,
I leave with more than when I came."

Place the coin in front of the candle and allow the candle to burn out on its own.

Bring your new talisman with you the next time you play games of chance.

LOST IS FOUND SPELL

Whether it's your keys, your phone, or something of less immediate importance, this spell can help you find your lost item.

Like any other magic, the most important aspect of this working is that you *believe* you will find what you have lost. If you keep your focus on the fact that you can't find it right this minute, then that will likely remain the case.

You will need:

- 2 silver candles
- 4-6 inch square of silver or black cloth

Instructions:

Place the cloth on your altar or work space, and place one candle on either side of it.

Light the candle to the left of the cloth, and state out loud what you are looking to find.

Now focus your attention on the cloth, and stare at it intently for at least 30 seconds.

Now close your eyes, and visualize the item you're seeking suddenly appearing, out of "nowhere," onto the cloth. See the item in as much detail as possible. Hold this vision steady for several moments.

When you feel ready, open your eyes and light the candle to the right of the cloth as you say the following (or similar) words:

"Lost is found, lost is found.
What I lost has just been found
and is on its way back to me.
It is done."

Fold up the cloth and place it somewhere on your altar, but in an inconspicuous place. You can tuck it under a crystal or candle, or simply place it off in a corner.

Gently extinguish the candles.

After the spell, trust that the item will come to you in perfect timing. When it does, you can shake out the cloth and return it to its regular place.

You can reuse the candles to repeat this spell for other lost items.

GOLD

Gold is the color of wheat fields, sunlight sparkling on water, and the precious metal that has been revered for thousands of years around the globe. A warm, optimistic, attractive color, gold holds the energy of the divine masculine, and the positive essence of aspiring to the highest standards.

Gold's properties make it excellent for magical workings related to success, achievement, confidence, courage, charm, and positive thinking. Its association with divine masculinity and with the mineral gold can be drawn upon for spellwork involving good fortune and abundance of all kinds, including financial wealth and prosperity.

Gold is even useful for manifesting luxury and extravagance, but it is more practically known for helping with better money management. Any matter involving happiness, blessings, or generosity is bound to benefit from the energies of this shining hue.

Gold also assists with connecting to the divine masculine in each person, regardless of gender. It can be used to boost inner strength, willpower, and intuition, and helps with the self-realization needed to heal emotional and psychic wounds from the past.

Workings related to any matter involving the need for justice, peace, and/or safety can benefit from the use of gold. This is a color of stability, which can be seen in the fact that the mineral gold, in its purest form, does not tarnish.

Gold is also useful in workings related to physical health, divination, and attracting good luck and money in a short amount of time. Some people also use gold candles during divination and for purification rituals.

Gold is a primary color of the God and is used to represent him on the Wiccan altar. It is associated with the Sun and with the Element of Fire, as well as the signs of Leo and Virgo. Its cardinal direction is South.

In the spells below, you'll work with the color gold to attract the energies of success, boost your ambition to achieve your goals, and increase your financial power, in the short and long term.

GOLDEN SCROLL SUCCESS SPELL

Whether you're facing a tough deadline, training to run a marathon, or taking on some other daunting task, the vibrations of the color gold can help you reach success in your endeavors.

This spell helps you to crystalize your focus on the alchemical blending of your own efforts with the support of the Universe. Use this spell for a boost of magical assistance from the higher realms any time you like!

<u>You will need:</u>

- 1 gold spell candle
- Bergamot, cinnamon, patchouli, ylang ylang, and/or lemon essential oil
- 1 or more work candles for atmosphere
- 1 piece goldstone or pyrite
- Slip of parchment or paper
- Several inches of gold thread
- Small cloth bag (optional)

<u>Instructions:</u>

Light the work candle(s). Anoint the gold spell candle with the oil.

Spend a few moments visualizing yourself succeeding at your goal. Imagine the feelings of relief, joy, triumph—whatever is appropriate for your situation—that you will experience once the goal is met.

Now consider what is needed from your end of things in order to meet the goal. For example, if you want to run a marathon, then diligent training will be required. If you're aiming to find a new job, then obviously you'll need to check job listings and polish up your resume.

Identify three actions you can take to "meet the Universe halfway" in your quest for success. Write these actions on the slip of parchment or paper, roll the paper into a scroll, and tie the gold thread around it.

Hold it gently between your palms as you say the following (or similar) words:

"I draw the energies of success
into and through my whole being.
I accomplish whatever I turn my attention to.
And so it is."

Now set the scroll in front of candle, holding it in place with the goldstone or pyrite. Allow the candle to burn out on its own.

You can place the scroll on your altar or carry it with you in a small cloth bag to remind you of your goal until it is accomplished.

GOLD AMBITION SPELL

When you're working your way up the ladder of success, you can sometimes lose sight of the big picture. If you're biding your time waiting for a promotion at a current job, considering a new career altogether, or wanting to strike out on your own in the world of self-employment, the energetic frequency of gold can help you boost your ambition to make the most out of your work.

You can use any size candle for this spell. If you'd like to repeat the spell for a few successive nights, use a pillar or taper candle so you can relight it each time.

<u>You will need:</u>

- 1 gold candle

- Bergamot, cinnamon, clove, patchouli, and/or lemon essential oil
- Crystal point, athame, or other ritual carving tool

Instructions:

Carve a symbol of your magical goal into the candle. This can be a "V" for victory, the rune Sowilo for success, a dollar sign, or a symbol that represents the kind of work you do (or want to be doing).

Take a few moments to envision how you want to feel about your work—whatever that may be. What does a successful day look like for you? What aspects of your work life can you see yourself being excited about? Visualize yourself filled with the energy of ambition, enthusiasm, and the drive to succeed.

When you have a strong hold on these positive feelings, light the candle as you say the following (or similar) words:

"Golden fire, golden flame—
ambition is my passion.
All is well above and below,
I am energized for action."

Now spend a few moments gazing at the candle. Visualize your energy going into the flame as it pushes up towards the sky.

Release any self-doubt or other negative thoughts or emotions that may have been draining your enthusiasm recently, and trust that you will soon be feeling the fire of ambition for your pursuits. Leave the candle to burn as long as you'd like.

PILE-OF-MONEY ABUNDANCE SPELL

Those who work consciously with the Law of Attraction know that *like attracts like*. The more we think about something, the more it shows up in our experience. The trick is to choose to focus positively rather than negatively. In other words, if we're focused on the *lack* of the thing we want, then we simply attract more *lack*.

All magic works via the Law of Attraction, but this spell enacts it in a very direct way, by creating a visual display of financial accumulation that can be used as a talisman to keep your thoughts about finances positive.

The denomination of coins you use isn't important, but for best results, use nine coins of the same or similar size. You may want to use nine pennies, as their copper color is close to the vibrational frequency of gold.

You will need:

- 1 gold candle
- Bergamot, cinnamon, and/or patchouli essential oil (optional)
- 9 same-sized coins
- Small cloth bag (optional)

Instructions:

Anoint the candle with the oil, if using.

Now light the candle, and as you allow some of the wax to melt, visualize yourself literally sitting or lying upon a gigantic pile of valuable gold coins.

Visualize the room entirely filled with gold coins, all of which are yours to do whatever you like with. (If you wish, you can include some paper money in your visualization—whatever you need to feel truly abundant in the most luxurious fashion possible.)

When enough wax has melted, place one coin on your altar or work space and drop a bead of wax on top of it.

Quickly place the next coin on top in order to "glue" them together. As you do this, visualize the room filling with even more gold coins (or paper dollars).

Repeat the process of dripping a bead of wax onto the coin and stacking another on top. Each time, visualize your finances expanding and increasing.

When all nine coins have been stacked on top of each other, hold the stack carefully in your hands and say the following (or similar) words:

"My growing wealth is represented here in my hands.
As positive energy builds upon itself, my money expands."

Place the "pile of money" on your altar, in your home office, or in the place where you conduct most of your financial business.

Each time you see it, quickly visualize the room filled with gold coins and express gratitude for the financial abundance in your life.

SEVEN-DAY MONEY MAGIC

This spell is great for anyone wanting to strengthen their money manifesting "muscles." While it may not bring you millions of dollars, if done properly it will definitely bring you confidence in your ability to work magic for tangible results.

The repetitive aspect of the spell—working it every night for a week—allows you to strengthen your visualization powers and take note of your results each day. To gain maximum benefit from the spell, keep a running journal of both the work and the results. You can even think of it as something like a science experiment, with cash rewards!

<u>You will need:</u>

- 1 gold pillar or taper candle
- Anointing oil (optional)
- Crystal point, athame, or other ritual carving tool
- Journal or writing paper

<u>Instructions:</u>

Notch a candle in seven sections by lightly carving complete circles around it.

Anoint the candle with the oil, if using.

Each night, for seven consecutive nights, burn a single section of the candle.

As the candle burns, focus your attention on the idea of discovering money in random ways as you go about your day.

This can be as simple as finding a penny on the ground, or more elaborate, like discovering a 20-dollar bill in a pair of pants you haven't worn in ages.

The specific scenario you envision doesn't matter—the point is to conjure up the feeling of surprise and delight that happens whenever we come up on money unexpectedly.

Hold on to this feeling for as long as you can. If you like, you can repeat the following (or similar) words as the candle burns:

"Money on the ground, money all around,
look at all the money I have just now found!"

After the candle has burned through its notch for the night, gently extinguish it, and record any impressions you may have had during the work.

At the end of the following day, record any results—even seemingly insignificant ones like finding a penny on the ground!

Then repeat the spell using the next notch on the candle. Follow this routine until the candle has burned through its last notch.

Be sure to look back through your notes to see all of your results. Do you see any patterns emerge? Any correlations between your personal energy during your nighttime visualizations and your results the following day? How can you apply what you've learned in this experiment to the rest of your magical practice?

BROWN

Next to green, brown is perhaps the earthiest of all colors. We see it in the soil, the bark of many trees, the fallen leaves at the end of autumn, and the mud that comes with spring.

Brown is also a color of the harvest, the time when we bring in the rewards of our summer labors and set up for a secure and abundant winter. For these reasons and more, brown is definitely a color of practicality—of being "down to Earth."

As such, brown is a highly effective color in magical workings related to plants, animals—wild and domestic, but especially companion animals and livestock—and anything else to do with Nature. This is a color of generosity, stability and security, especially as it relates to the home, and it is often used in house-blessing rituals. Brown is useful for material gain of all kinds, and is excellent for spellwork focused on food and food security. It is also a go-to color for assistance with financial crises.

Brown is also associated with friendships, and is used in magic relating to trust, honesty, sincerity, and loyalty between friends. Its grounding and centering properties make it useful for balancing intense emotions, providing emotional support, and promoting strength and endurance. It aids with making decisions from a practical standpoint rather than emotional attachments, and reigns in indecisiveness.

Brown's steady, practical energies can be harnessed to strengthen or solidify developments already underway, particularly if they relate to real estate or construction. It is very helpful for situations requiring concentration and focus, such as studying for exams, and for finding lost items.

Brown is associated with both the planet and the Element of Earth, as well as the signs of Scorpio and Capricorn. Its cardinal direction is North.

In the spells below, the properties of brown are harnessed to help you get a garden off to a magical start, foster concentration while working on a large project, find a companion animal to join you on your life's journey, and promote balance in all aspects of your life.

GARDEN SEED BLESSING SPELL

Whether you're planting a full-fledged garden or just growing some herbs in pots on your window sill, this spell will give your plants a boost as they grow from tiny seeds into vibrant flowers, herbs, and/or vegetables.

You can work the spell for one packet of seeds at a time, but it will work just as well for all of your season's seeds in one go. Happy planting!

You will need:

- 2 brown spell candles
- 1 work candle for atmosphere
- Seed packet(s)

Instructions:

Light the work candle.

Arrange the seed packets in a pleasing manner (e.g. in a triangle or circle if you have enough packets) on your altar or work space.

Place one spell candle to either side of the seeds.

Light the spell candle to the left of the seeds.

Visualize the seeds beginning to stir under the surface of the soil. Watch as the first green shoots begin to reach for the surface and emerge into the open air. See the shoots continue to grow, pulsing with life force energy, as they allow themselves to be nourished by sunlight and water, until they are fully mature plants.

Visualize yourself enjoying your plants, whether through harvesting their nourishment or simply appreciating their beauty.

When you have reached this stage of the visualization, light the candle to the right of the seeds as you say the following (or similar) words:

"As above, so below,
I watch joyfully as you grow.
As below, so above,
these seeds are blessed with divine love."

Allow the candles to burn out on their own, and then plant your seeds.

FOCUS AND CONCENTRATION SPELL

Being fully focused is an enjoyable and fulfilling experience. Whether you're working on a school project, a hobby you're passionate about, or even a presentation for work, there's nothing better than losing yourself in the task—without distractions, without resistance, without even an awareness of time.

This simple spell draws on brown's vibrational frequencies to keep you focused and "in the zone" until the project is successfully completed. You may even finish the job in less time than you thought it would take!

For best results, work this spell at your desk or other work space, rather than your altar, since you'll want the candle burning near you as you work on your task.

<u>You will need:</u>

- 1 brown taper or pillar candle
- Ylang ylang, peppermint, or lemon essential oil

Instructions:

Anoint the candle with the oil, and spend a few moments quieting your mind.

Visualize the zone of focus you wish to experience through your task today.

When you're ready, take a deep breath and light the candle.

Now get to work, trusting that the Universe will bring you the focused energy you need to manifest your intention.

When you have completed the project (or the time you have to spend on the project), extinguish the candle.

Re-light the candle to re-enter the "zone" the next time you work on the project, or any time you need an extra boost of focus.

SPELL FOR FINDING YOUR COMPANION ANIMAL

While many people may think of their dogs and cats as "pets," those in the Witching world understand that a better term is "companion animal," since these animals are sentient beings in their own right. If you are planning to bring a companion animal into your life, it would be ideal to consider adopting from a shelter, since there are so many animals in need of loving homes.

The following spell can help you find the guidance you need for choosing your companion animal—or for being in the right place at the right time for your companion to choose you!

You will need:

- 1 brown spell candle or tea light
- Juniper, lavender, palmarosa, rose, and/or vetiver essential oil (optional)
- Crystal point, athame, or other ritual carving tool

Instructions:

Spend several minutes quieting your mind, through deep breathing, meditation, listening to calming music, or all of the above. The objective is to get into a space where you will be able to receive messages and impulses from the spiritual realm.

When you feel centered, carve a heart shape (or other symbol that represents love for you) into the candle. Then, anoint the candle with the oil, if using.

Now spend a few moments visualizing how you will feel when you have your companion animal beside you.

Feel the warmth of the animal beside you (or in your lap). Feel the soft fur/hair of the animal in your hand.

As you sink into this visualization, take note of any specific impressions that arise, such as the animal's size, color, sounds, textures, even possible names. (Don't worry if nothing specific comes to mind—just take note if it does.) Summon the feeling of joyful, unconditional love between you and your companion animal.

When you feel ready, light the candle and say the following words:

"I am ready to greet you, my loving friend. Thank you for sharing your life with me."

Allow the candle to burn all the way down, and have confidence that you will know your new companion as soon as you see her/him.

BALANCE AND STABILITY SPELL

Witches who raise energy as part of their ritual practice understand the importance of "Earthing," or grounding excess energy once the magical work has been completed. It's not only in ritual, however, that we can end up with more energy—whether it feels positive or negative— than is ideal for us to live balanced, stable lives.

This simple yet elegant spell uses the grounding energies of brown, as well as the literal Earth, to help draw out excess energy and rebalance body and mind. Try this anytime you feel out of sorts, or make it a regular practice—remember that the Earth is always good for you!

Ideally, this spell is worked outdoors on grass, sand, or some other flat area in Nature. If this isn't possible, then gather some soil from an outdoor area to use inside.

<u>You will need:</u>

- 4 brown tea lights or votive candles
- Outdoor area or pot of soil from the Earth

<u>Instructions:</u>

Find a quiet space outside and place the candles one in each cardinal direction (North, East, South, West), with enough room for you to fit inside the circle. Light each candle, starting in the North and moving clockwise.

When the candles are lit, sit in the middle of the circle. Place your hands directly on the earth and focus on releasing any negative energy while absorbing positive energy. Feel your body balance as the exchange of energy takes place.

Sit in this position for at least 5 minutes, but try to stay for longer, up to 30 minutes. When you feel grounded and balanced, thank the Earth for her healing energies and gently extinguish the candles.

GREY

The color of cloudy skies and rainy days, grey is often perceived to be a gloomy color. However, it can also be a welcome counterbalance against too much fiery energy from a long stretch of hot, sunny weather. The ultimate color of neutrality, grey helps us to take a step back, cool off a bit, slow down, and go inward. Grey is also the color of stone, and its energies are likewise solid, stable, strong, enduring, and ancient.

As the midpoint between white and black, grey contains properties associated with each. It is useful for magic relating to psychic ability, dreams, and intuition, as well as protection from negativity and binding, removing, or neutralizing negative influences. Grey is the quintessential color of balance, and can help whenever matters arise that challenge one's sense of serenity and composure.

It helps one maintain a calm reserve and patience when dealing with unknown outcomes, and with endurance during difficult circumstances. Grey also helps with releasing attachments to people, situations, and outcomes, and can soothe loneliness.

Grey is also used by some in "glamour" magic, to appear more appealing to others in any number of ways. It can be used in order to be treated with more respect, or to become "invisible," meaning that people you don't want to interact with won't notice you. The only caveat in this type of magic is to focus on the energy you project outward, rather than trying to control what other people think.

Use grey in workings related to complex decisions and other situations that require impartiality, discernment, contemplation, and objective observation and analysis. It is particularly excellent for neutralizing volatile or fiery conflicts, and resolving any situations that require compromise.

Grey is associated with the Moon and with the signs of Virgo, Scorpio, Cancer, and Capricorn. Its Elemental association is Water and its cardinal direction is West.

In this chapter, you'll find spells to help you avoid interacting with grouchy people, neutralize negative influences in your life, resolve a conflict, and see your way through an important decision.

ANTI-GROUCH INVISIBILITY SPELL

We've all had the experience of starting off in a great mood, only to be brought down by the grumblings and complaints of other people we encounter during our day.

This isn't necessarily intentional on their part—often they subconsciously interpret our happy vibes as an invitation to vent, in hopes that they will feel better after talking to us. However, the result is usually the opposite, as we simply end up sinking down to their lower vibration, while they stay focused on their unhappiness.

This spell utilizes the "cloaking" powers of the color grey to make you "invisible" to those whose negativity might otherwise cause them to latch on to your light. While they may still physically see you, you won't appear to be someone they want to unload on, leaving you free to cultivate your happy mood unobstructed.

You will need:

- 1 grey spell candle
- Cedarwood, clove, juniper, or vetiver essential oil (optional)

Instructions:

Anoint the candle with the oil, if using.

Spend a few moments cultivating a feeling of appreciation and gratitude for all that is going well in your life.

State these positive elements out loud, and aim for a list of at least 20. (These can be specific or general. They can be very simple things that you've recently experienced, like a smile from a child on the street or a nice meal, or long-term things like good health or a safe place to live.)

Now light the candle and take a few deep breaths. Visualize yourself walking through your day.

As you approach the vicinity of someone in a bad mood, see a grey mist covering you from head to toe, so that the person merely steps past you without realizing you're there.

At the same time, know that people with higher vibrational frequencies can still see you, and even share their positive energy with you whenever you cross paths. Summon up the feeling of well-being that comes from spending quality time with positive people, and the freedom from draining conversations that don't serve you.

When you feel confidently cloaked from any unwanted interactions, say the following (or similar) words:

"Now you see me, now you don't.
If you're happy, you'll see me,
if you're not, you won't!"

Gently extinguish the candle.

If you like, you can repeat this spell with the same candle until it is spent.

NEGATIVE INFLUENCE NEUTRALIZER

While magic can help you eliminate negative energy from your environment and even dodge interactions with negative people (such as the Anti-Grouch Invisibility Spell above), sometimes there are unpleasant situations and people you simply can't avoid.

However, you don't have to get bogged down in the negativity surrounding the person or situation. This spell helps you to neutralize that negative energy so that it doesn't influence your thoughts or mood.

It's important to keep your focus not on individual people or conflicts, but on neutralizing the feelings they activate in you that you wish to be free from.

This is the best way to "do no harm" and avoid unintended consequences from your magic. It's also the most efficient way to improve your own circumstances, as you will be both neutralizing the negative influences and raising your vibrational frequency at the same time, which will reduce your chances of attracting negativity in general.

Depending on the size of your heat-proof dish, you may want to keep a small amount of water on hand just to be on the safe side.

<u>You will need:</u>

- 1 grey candle
- Small slip(s) of paper
- Glass bowl or other heat-proof dish
- Small cup of water (optional)

<u>Instructions:</u>

Light the candle as you say the following (or similar) words:

"I welcome transformational energy of the fire and now neutralize the following negative influences. So let it be."

On a slip of paper, write a single influence that you would like to banish. For example, you might write "the negativity surrounding this interpersonal conflict," or "the unease when I walk into my workplace," or "the feeling I get when someone complains to me."

Then fold the paper in half.

Carefully light the paper using the flame from the candle as you say the following (or similar) words:

"With harm to none, this energy is now returned to the Earth. It is done."

Place the burning paper in the glass dish.

As it continues to burn, visualize the negative influence being pulled out of your life and buried deep within the healing Earth.

Trust that the energy is now neutralized, clearing space within your vibrational field to attract more positivity into your life.

If you like, you can repeat this process with more negative influences, using more slips of paper.

When you are done, extinguish the candle. Take the ashes from the paper outside and bury them in the Earth.

CONFLICT RESOLUTION SPELL

Disagreements between two people are rarely completely cut and dry; often both people have salient points and good reasons for their thoughts and opinions about the subject at hand. With compassion and an open mind, it is always possible to come to a compromise that respects all parties involved. This spell can give you a big boost in that direction.

Note: before working this spell, make sure you have released any attachments to being "right," or to controlling the outcome in some way (such as needing the other person to "surrender" and agree with you completely). Otherwise, you risk being manipulative with your magical energy, which can easily backfire!

<u>You will need:</u>

- 1 grey spell candle
- Bergamot, lavender, palmarosa, rose, and/or ylang ylang essential oil
- Crystal point, athame, or other ritual carving tool

<u>Instructions:</u>

Take some time to ground and center.

When you're ready, carve your initials into one side of the candle.

Carve the initials of the person you're in conflict with into the other side, and then anoint the candle with the oil.

Spend a few moments focusing your attention on qualities you respect in the other person.

Make a mental list and strive for at least ten positive attributes about the person. If your thoughts wander to the argument or conflict, gently redirect them back into positive territory.

Now focus your attention on yourself. Make a mental list of at least ten aspects of yourself that you respect and are proud of. Note that some of these are likely to be on the other person's list as well.

When you feel a sense of peace and calm objectivity begin to take hold, light the candle as you say the following (or similar) words:

"Compassion, respect, and understanding bring peace.
Let resolution come, and harmony reign.
Blessed Be."

Now release the conflict from your mind, trusting the Universe to respond to your focused intention with perfect timing.

Gently extinguish the candle, and know that the opportunity to resolve the conflict peacefully will soon present itself.

BIG DECISION BRANCH-OUT SPELL

When you've got a complex or monumental choice to make, especially one that seems cloudy or is causing you anxiety, grey is the optimal color for accessing a calm, neutral space from which to contemplate your options. This spell creates a magical brainstorming experience, in which you go beyond a "pros and cons" approach in a clear and focused way.

The tree here serves as a visual metaphor, so that you can view the range of possible outcomes all in one place. The branches represent the various pathways or outcomes that are likely to result from your possible choices. The trunk of the tree remains firmly in the ground, just as you will remain grounded as you consider the varied paths toward your future.

<u>You will need:</u>

- 1 large grey pillar candle
- Cinnamon, lavender, palmarosa, or peppermint essential oil (optional)
- Crystal point, athame, or other ritual carving tool
- Blank, unlined sheet of paper
- Journal or writing paper
- Grey pencil or marker

<u>Instructions:</u>

Spend a few moments quieting your mind. Don't think about your situation yet, but rather focus on your breathing and let go of extraneous thoughts.

On the front of the candle, carve an image of a large tree with many branches. As you create the tree, focus your intention on enjoying an anxiety-free time to peacefully ponder your next move, trusting your inner wisdom to come through in this time and place. Then anoint the candle with the oil (if using).

Light the candle and with the pencil or marker draw a similar many-branched tree on the unlined paper.

For each possible choice involved in your decision, label a branch. For example, if you're trying to choose a new city to live in, name a branch for each place you're considering. If you're looking to solve a problem at work, label a branch for each possible solution you've thought of.

On another page in your journal, begin to write about the possible results of each choice. Don't be overly methodical about this—rather, start with whichever branch has the most energy for you in this moment. Freewrite about what you envision manifesting through this choice. Then move on to the next branch that you feel drawn to contemplate.

You may or may not arrive at a definitive answer by the end of this session, but you will have a clearer sense of where you're headed and much less anxiety about the question. Some decisions may take several days to work through, and new information or circumstances may shift your perspective on the matter. If so, you can always repeat the spell, with the same candle or a new one.

PINK

Pink is a quintessential color of love, with the fiery, passionate energies of red tempered by the higher vibrations of white. Seen in many types of flowers and blossoms, as well as in the sky at sunrise and sunset, pink exudes a cheerful, gentle, feminine energy that can be harnessed for many magical purposes relating to positive emotions and well-being.

Pink is the ideal candle color for all matters related to love, whether it's romantic, familial, the love between friends, or the ever-important love of self. It is associated with romance, passion, and sensuality, but its energies also encompass affection, kindness, compassion, and honor. Use pink in workings related to any situation that calls for the care and nurturing of others, and in any situation where you're finding it difficult to "do the right thing."

Pink's peaceful energies make it excellent for magic focused on friendship, companionship, and partnerships of all kinds. It is useful for manifesting and maintaining harmony—especially harmony within the home and within one's self. This includes spellwork related to forgiveness and reconciliation, and to spiritual and emotional healing.

For those who truly resonate with this color, it can be the ultimate aid in raising one's vibrational frequency, and can also assist with increasing physical energy. As a color of new beginnings, pink can contribute to success in all kinds of self-improvement endeavors.

Although it has been considered a color for "girls" since the mid-20th century, pink is actually associated with children and babies in general, and can be used in spellwork related to their health and protection, as well as workings for children to participate in. Pink is excellent for manifesting calm and relaxation, particularly when approaching a potentially frightening experience such as surgery.

Pink is associated with the planet Venus and the sign of Aries. Its Elemental association is Fire and its cardinal direction is South.

In this chapter, pink is used in a delightful spell to be worked with children, a spell to strengthen friendship, a magical romance recipe, and a ritual for strengthening self-love.

A SPELL FOR CHILDREN TO START THE DAY

Here's a spell you can teach your children to give their day a magical boost. It's great to do after breakfast and before everyone leaves for work and school, but you may want to first try it on a weekend morning, when time is more flexible. You can tell the children you're going to teach them a magic spell to make the day extra special.

All you need are a candle, pink chalk, and a patch of sidewalk or other concrete area to draw on. Depending on the age of the children, you may want to use an LED candle in lieu of actual flame.

<u>You will need:</u>

- 1 pink pillar candle
- Pink sidewalk chalk
- Sidewalk or other suitable concrete area

<u>Instructions:</u>

Begin by standing in a circle, with about two feet of space between each person.

Have each child trace their footprints on the ground with the chalk. Trace your own, too, if you like!

If there are only 2 or 3 people working the spell, then have each child trace their footprints twice to make a circle at least 4 feet in diameter.

When the chalk footprint circle is completed, place the candle in the center. Now pick a starting point on the circle facing East (the direction of beginnings).

Instruct the children to jump from one set of footprints to the next. As they jump they should shout out the following (or similar) words:

"Good fun, great day!
Magic powers light the way!"

Have them stop at each footprint and say one thing they want to go well that day, whether it's a test at school, having fun during playground time, getting along with friends, or enjoying the movie you're going to see.

When everyone (yourself included!) has jumped around the circle and spoken their intentions for the day, have each person return to standing in their drawn footprints, facing the candle in the center.

Carefully light the candle and then have everyone hold hands and repeat the spell words three times in unison.

Allow the children to gently blow out the candle. You can reuse the candle anytime you want to repeat the spell.

At the end of the day, ask the children what their favorite moments of the day were, and look for connections between their stated intentions that morning and the manifestations that unfolded over the course of the day.

FRIENDSHIP-STRENGTHENING SPELL

Sometimes even the best of friends can end up on the outs for no clear reason.

Whether you're dealing with communication difficulties, tensions from unknown causes, or a flat-out rift, this spell can help repair the strains that sometimes arise among friends. Drawing specifically on the combined vibrations of red and white, the spell seeks to temper passion with peace as you celebrate the strengths of both yourself and your friend.

Note: as with any spell involving another person, be sure your focus is on the desired outcome, rather than on magically manipulating another person's behavior. Otherwise, you run the risk of making the situation even worse!

You will need:

- 2 pink votives or tea lights
- Work candle for atmosphere
- Small amount of red and white paints
- 1 paint brush
- 5-inch square of pink poster board or card stock

Instructions:

Light the work candle and arrange the rest of the spell ingredients on your altar or work space.

Place the poster board or card stock in the center and then place one pink candle to either side of it, leaving enough space for you to work with the paints and brush.

Light the candle to the left of the poster board as you say the following (or similar) words:

"Let the light and love of friendship
shine throughout this work.
So let it be."

Using the white paint, paint a heart (or some other symbol of your friendship) onto the poster board.

Then, without rinsing the brush, swirl red paint into the white shape, to create the color pink.

While you swirl the red and white paint together, visualize a reconciliation with your friend. See the two of you laughing and having a good time together, and allow yourself to feel the way you do when you're enjoying time with this friend.

When the heart (or other shape) is completely pink, set down the paintbrush and light the candle to the right of the poster board as you say the following (or similar) words:

"The light and love of friendship
seals this working and strengthens our bond.
So let it be."

Allow the candles to burn while the paint dries. Then gently extinguish them and place the painting on your altar or in another specially designated location.

Trust that the opportunity to strengthen or repair the friendship will arrive in perfect timing.

STRAWBERRY SALAD ROMANCE SPELL

This fun bit of kitchen witchery utilizes the potent romantic vibrations of pink. It's designed to attract a new romance, but can also be used to spice up an existing one.

Just make sure your magical intent is on the romantic experiences you want to have, rather than on the specific behavior of another person—otherwise the spell is likely to backfire!

As you prepare this cheerful fruit salad, be sure to focus your intention into the individual ingredients, as well as the process itself. Give your magic a boost by playing some fun, romantic music, burning some special incense or essential oils, and any other atmospheric enhancement that will help you keep your focus on manifesting romance through the power of Earth's delicious blessings.

Feel free to tailor the recipe to your liking. You can add and/or remove ingredients, tweak the amounts called for, etc. For best results, however, strive to keep pink as the dominant color of the salad.

This recipe makes approximately two servings and will keep for two days tightly covered in the refrigerator.

You will need:

- 2 pink candles
- Work candle for atmosphere (preferably pink or red)
- 2 cups strawberries, halved
- 1 cup raspberries
- 1 cup watermelon, chopped into bite-sized pieces
- ½ cup blueberries and/or blackberries
- ½ cup cherries, pitted
- 1 and ½ tablespoons fresh mint or basil leaves, chopped
- 3 teaspoons fresh squeezed lemon juice
- 1 and ½ teaspoons maple syrup or honey

Instructions:

Light the work candle and begin rinsing and chopping the fresh ingredients. If you like, you can imagine that you're preparing this dish for your new romantic partner.

Place all of the fruit in a bowl and stir in the mint or basil leaves, continuing to focus on your romantic desires.

In a small bowl or ramekin, whisk together the lemon juice and maple syrup or honey.

Pour on top of the fruit salad and mix gently until all the fruit is evenly coated with the dressing.

Now light the pink candles and say the following or similar words:

"This sweet and bountiful food, so lovingly prepared,
brings forth the abundant essence of new love in my life.
So let it be."

Sit down and enjoy your enchanted strawberry creation!

As you do, continue to visualize the experiences of romance that you're seeking. What kind of person are you looking for? What will you talk about, where will you go, and how will you feel when you're together?

Enjoy fantasizing about your upcoming romance until you're finished enjoying your salad.

Put away any leftovers and gently extinguish the candles. You can relight them when you're entertaining your new romantic partner in your home!

SEVEN-DAY SELF-LOVE SPELL

In modern Western culture, the idea of self-love is often confused with selfishness, egotistical behavior. But the truth is that without loving ourselves, we're setting ourselves up for unhealthy relationships with others, as well as a wide range of disappointments in life.

Cultivating the vibrational frequency of self-love is arguably the most powerful kind of magic there is. This spell won't instantly remove all your blocks to loving yourself, but it can get you well established on the path toward profound emotional and spiritual healing.

You will need:

- 1 pink seven-day candle
- Journal or writing paper
- Mirror

Instructions:

Spend several minutes in quiet meditation. You may want to try the Indigo Zone Meditation Practice, above, or another brief grounding and centering technique.

When you're ready, light the candle. Spend several minutes freewriting about the idea of self-love.

What feels difficult or even unwanted about this concept? What might be blocking you from embracing the idea of loving yourself? Do you feel you have to have achieved specific things in order to deserve it, like losing weight, getting all your homework done, or being extraordinarily talented at something?

What if you could love yourself no matter what you look like, no matter what you do or don't do on any given day? What do you imagine an experience of true self-love might feel like?

There are no correct answers here—simply write openly and honestly about your relationship with yourself, and what you would like to see develop from this point.

When you're finished writing, pick up the mirror and look your reflection in the eyes.

Say out loud, to yourself, "I love you," three times.

Don't worry if this feels silly or even unpleasant—these are normal reactions at first. Say the words anyway, being sure to look yourself in the eye.

(Note, if you don't have a portable mirror, you can do this step in front of any mounted mirror.)

Allow the candle to burn out on its own, which typically takes seven days. At least once each day, make a point of looking in the mirror and saying "I love you" to yourself, three times.

Every time you notice the candle, remind yourself that you are worth this magical work, just by virtue of being alive and being yourself.

Take note of any shifts in your emotional, spiritual, and even physical experiences during this period. Consider maintaining the mirror ritual for at least thirty days, and note how it gets easier over time.

CONCLUSION

As you explore and develop your practice of candle magic, you will be strengthening your relationship with the Element of Fire, and with the infinite possibilities contained within the vibrational frequencies of the visible light spectrum.

If you keep track of your spellwork in a Book of Shadows or a journal, you may discover over time that certain colors produce more powerful results for you than others. This may be because you prefer certain colors on an aesthetic level, or because elements of your personal vibrational frequency tend to resonate with those colors. Either way, it can be a delightful process to develop your own preferred magical "color palette," building on your prior experience with a few choice colors and expanding into related shades and hues.

However, don't focus too narrowly on a small handful of colors, or you may miss out on new magical discoveries. Branch out from time to time and try a spell with a color you don't automatically resonate with. You may be surprised at what new experiences these less familiar colors can bring into your life!

As a final reminder, feel free to use any of these spells as a template from which to design your own, and always follow the wisdom of your inner Witch. And no matter what, use caution—it is important to remember and respect the destructive capacities of Fire. Enjoy your journey with the magic of candles. Here's to a vibrant, multicolored, warm and illuminating magical life!

WICCA

BOOK OF CRYSTAL SPELLS

A Beginner's Book of Shadows for Wiccans, Witches, and Other Practitioners of Crystal Magic

LISA CHAMBERLAIN

CONTENTS

INTRODUCTION

Welcome to my *Book of Crystal Spells*!

Crystals have been used in magic for centuries, in many cultures throughout the world. The ancients often wore them for protection, good luck, prosperity, and other purposes. Today, Witches, healers, and many others understand that crystals are "alive" in their own way, capable of communicating their ancient wisdom with us if we are open and receptive to their messages. They seem to speak silently of the infinite, creative, living power of the Earth.

This collection of spells, rituals, and other workings is devoted to the magical energies of crystals and other mineral stones*, and can be used on its own or as a companion to my dedicated book on the topic, *Crystal Magic*. Each spell is relatively simple and suitable for beginners to magic, yet can inspire more seasoned practitioners as well.

Many of these spells are focused on aspects of emotional healing and energetic balancing, two purposes that crystals are uniquely suited for. As such, single crystals are often the focus of these spells, with minimal additional ingredients, in order to help you deepen your own magical relationships with these powerful ancient tools.

The spells are even organized by stone, rather than by purpose or form, in order to give you an opportunity to work closely with different types of crystals, one at a time. Of course, other more traditional magical goals are also represented here, including protection from various unwanted circumstances and personal empowerment in the face of challenges, as well as prosperity and healthy relationships. For readers of *Crystal Magic*, all 13 stones will be familiar, though some new information about each is featured here, in addition to the new spells.

Crystals can be found anywhere you purchase magical supplies, as well as in shops devoted entirely to minerals. Some gift stores in science museums also sell tumbled or raw specimens of crystals and minerals, and can be a great place to find stones that are local to the region.

No matter where you acquire your crystals, be sure to thoroughly cleanse them of old, residual energies before using them. Methods for cleansing crystals include running water over them for several minutes, and burying them in salt or soil overnight. You can also bury them in the Earth overnight.

The next step is to charge your crystals. Most crystals and minerals can be charged in sunlight, though a few, such as amethyst and rose quartz, will fade in color if left in the sun for too long. Moonlight is an excellent alternative for these (and all) stones.

Be sure to cleanse and charge your crystals on a regular basis, especially those you use often in spellwork. This is especially important for stones used to absorb negative energy, such as jet and black tourmaline. You can find more detailed information about clearing and charging your crystals in *Crystal Magic*.

For people new to spellwork, a few more practical tips are worth reiterating here. First, please note that the instructions for each spell assume that you have already charged your stones and other ingredients for the specific magical purpose you are working for. If you haven't yet learned to charge magical items, research and try a few different methods until you find what feels most appropriate for you.

One approach is to lay the stones on a pentacle slab, or simply hold them between your palms, and speak words of intention related to the spellwork you'll be doing. Depending on your practice, you might invoke the Goddess and God, the Elements, or other spiritual energies you work with.

As for candles, which appear often in these pages, some spells include instructions for what to do with the candle when the spell is over, while others do not. If it's left unspecified, you can choose to leave the candle burning or snuff it out gently (with a candle snuffer or by waving your hand). You can use the candle again for atmospheric lighting, or for repeats of the same spell, but avoid reusing candles for different spells altogether.

Finally, always remember that no matter the size, amount, or appearance of your crystals, or how closely you follow the spell instructions, your state of mind is the chief factor in any successful spellwork. Approach a spell with doubt that it will work, and you've pretty much guaranteed that it won't. Approach it with anxiety, and you're likely to get mixed results or no results at all.

The most successful magic is done from a place of calm centeredness and with very focused intent. So always do whatever you need to do to get grounded, whether that's through meditation, visualization, breathing techniques, a ritual circle-casting, or all of the above. Many of these spells include reminders to spend time quieting your mind, but it's up to you to take this step before any magical working. It is ultimately *your* energy that's shifting the reality of the Universe, so shape it well and use it wisely!

It is my hope that you find many useful workings in this crystal Book of Shadows, and that it will help you develop your own magical relationships with these beautiful and powerful gifts from the Earth.

Blessed Be.

**A note on terminology: "crystal" and "stone" are used interchangeably in this book. This is because the technical differences between the two isn't significant when it comes to magic. Actually, the more appropriate term in many cases is "mineral," as opposed to "crystal," since not every stone associated with magic has the kind of orderly molecular structure that characterizes a "true" crystal.*

QUARTZ CRYSTAL

Often thought of as the "quintessential" crystal, quartz is the second most abundant mineral on Earth, and one of the most common stones you will find in magical supply shops.

Comprised of just two elements—silicon and oxygen—it runs in color from completely "crystal clear" to milky white. Clear quartz is found as a six-sided prism and is often used in schools to demonstrate the ability of a mineral to hold the entire spectrum of light—held in sunlight, the prism will transmit rainbow patterns onto floors and walls.

The Aztecs, Egyptians, Romans, and many other ancient cultures used quartz in a multitude of ways that ranged from meditations to funerary rites. Among ancient lunar-aligned stone circles in Scotland, for example, lumps of white quartz were ritually broken and scattered, which may have mimicked the moonlight shining down on the participants. And according to some interpretations, quartz is among the "seven precious substances" of Buddhism. Today, it is widely used in alternative healing modalities as well as magic of various kinds.

Known to some as "the Witch's mirror," quartz is associated with both the Moon and the Sun and the Elements of Water and Fire. This stone is a potent tool for storing energy in the form of thoughts, memories and emotions, and can be easily "programmed" to activate previously stored energy when called upon. Quartz is often used to charge magical tools and spell ingredients, and can even be used to energetically cleanse other crystals and stones.

Quartz is also considered the "sage" of all minerals as it most easily facilitates the merging of the physical and spiritual realms. This is, after all, the original substance that crystal balls are made from!

Quartz absorbs and transmits energy from the Sun as well as from the life force of trees, plants and flowers, and like several other crystals it can be used to revitalize struggling plants around the home. Quartz is a great all-around rebalancing stone, replacing negative energies with positive ones and keeping harmonious vibrations going strong in any area where it resides.

In this chapter, you'll learn how to use quartz for storing and retrieving memories, energizing divination tools, improving your health, and boosting your energy toward achieving a specific goal.

CRYSTAL DIVINATION RECALIBRATOR

Quartz is often used to charge ritual and magical tools. As a stone of spiritual communication and psychic ability, it's ideal for sprucing up your divination tools—such as Tarot cards, runes, a pendulum, etc.—whenever you can sense their energy has become "fuzzy" or imbalanced in some way. In fact, many Tarot practitioners like to keep a quartz crystal with their Tarot cards at all times, to keep the energy of the deck in tip-top shape.

Technically, you can use any size crystal with any type of divination tools, but it's best to "match" the two as closely as possible. For example, a small crystal point may work well when rebalancing a pendulum, but when it comes to a Tarot deck or bag of runes, a more sizable crystal is ideal.

<u>You will need:</u>

- 1 medium to large quartz crystal
- White candle
- Divination tool(s)

<u>Instructions:</u>

Light the candle and spend a few moments quieting your mind.

When you're ready, place the divination tool in your left hand and the quartz in your right hand.

Gently bring them together until they touch.

Holding them together for at least one minute, visualize the divination tool being cleared of any unwanted energy, and then revitalized with the pure energy of the quartz.

When you feel that the recalibration is complete, thank the quartz and place your divination tool on the altar.

Repeat the procedure with any other divination tools you want to rebalance.

When you have finished, gently extinguish the white candle.

CRYSTAL QUARTZ MEMENTO CHARM

As computer researchers have been discovering, quartz has the ability to store information, or "data," in the form of energy. But it also stores emotional information, which makes this crystal an excellent touchstone for positive memories that you want to hold onto.

This spell is a great one for experimenting with the energetic properties of quartz. Simply select a happy memory—whether recent or from the distant past—and charge the stone with the feelings it brings out in you.

Note: this works best with pure clear quartz, so try to find as clear a stone as possible.

You will need:

- 1 clear quartz crystal
- White, pink or yellow candle
- Journal or writing paper (optional)

Instructions:

Light the candle and spend some time quieting your mind.

Begin to recall the memory in as much detail as you can. If it's a memory from the past, you may want to spend 10 to 15 minutes writing about it, as this is guaranteed to bring up details you may not be able to access otherwise.

When you have a good grasp on the memory, take the quartz and hold it between your palms.

With your eyes closed, visualize every possible sensory detail about the memory—sights, sounds, tastes, noises, voices, your thoughts and feelings at the time, etc. Focus on the feelings that accompanied this memory and feel them again in the present moment.

Continue the visualization until you feel suffused with warm, positive energy. Then place the quartz in front of the candle, leaving it for at least one hour.

Now you can hold the quartz whenever you want to call up this memory and feel the positive emotions you've infused the stone with. You can place it on your altar or somewhere else where you'll see it often, or carry it with you in your pocket or purse.

CRYSTAL ELIXIR FOR PHYSICAL HEALTH

Crystal elixirs—the infusing of water with the vibrations of crystals and other mineral stones—have been used for healing purposes since at least 3000 B.C.E. in various cultures. These simple, magical potions work through the body's direct absorption of the vibrations of the crystal, creating an alignment between your own energy and that of the stone chosen for the particular purpose.

The rebalancing powers of quartz crystal can be used to bring about physical regeneration and revitalization in the body by working at the subtle energy level. This elixir is great for those who have been feeling low on energy, are recovering from a minor illness, or would simply like an all-around rebalancing "lift" of healing energy.

Note: Some crystals and stones are highly toxic, and should never be used internally in any way. So if you're wanting to explore this particular magical technique further, be sure to do thorough research on any stone you're considering for use in an elixir!

You will need:

- 1 small piece of clear quartz
- Cup of filtered water

Instructions:

Place the quartz in a small glass of water and leave it in the sunshine for one day. The following day, perform the healing ritual.

Remove the quartz from the water carefully and place it on your altar or table. Keep the water in the center of your altar or table.

Take three deep breaths to relax and focus.

Take a moment to meditate on your body. Allow your mind to scan your body from the top of your head down to your feet. Notice any areas that may need attention.

Return to the first place you noticed an imbalance in your body. Focus on healing that area as you take a sip of the water.

Visualize the power and ancient wisdom of the quartz healing that area, releasing any tension, discomfort, or other unwanted sensations.

Repeat this with each area of your body that needs attention and healing.

When you are finished, allow yourself a moment to feel the vibration of the quartz throughout your body, healing and reviving your being.

You can repeat this ritual whenever your body needs a boost of healing energy.

ENERGY AMPLIFIER FOR REACHING A GOAL

When your heart is set on a significant goal, quartz is a powerful magical ally to help you literally crystallize your will and intent. Whether it's related to love, career, health or spiritual development, quartz can accelerate the fulfillment of your desires by amplifying the energy that is programmed into it.

As you perform this spell, it is important to not only consider the end result of your goal but to direct the energies of feeling successful and satisfied with your manifestation into the stone.

You will need:

- 1 pure clear quartz crystal
- Small slip of paper
- Small drawstring bag

Instructions:

Spend some time quieting your mind.

Focus on the goal you have made for yourself.

Write your goal on the small slip of paper. Remember to be very specific about what you would like to attain, as this will help concentrate the energy on the outcome you desire. For example, if the goal is a new job, don't simply write "new job." Focus on the type of job you want, and write a brief but specific description.

Wrap the quartz in the slip of paper.

Hold the paper and the quartz in your hands.

Concentrate on your goal by visualizing it being completed. How will you feel? What consequences or effects will the outcome have on your life?

When you have conjured the most detailed and positive visualization that you can, place the paper-wrapped quartz in the drawstring bag and tie it shut, while saying the following (or similar) words:

"With stone of Earth and power of Fire
I manifest my heart's desire"

Place the quartz where it can be close to you in your activities for completing the goal. This could be on your desk, in your purse, in your car, on top of your computer, or in a room in your house.

Repeat this spell with a new goal and a new quartz whenever you need.

ROSE QUARTZ

Widely beloved for its cheerful yet calming pink hues, rose quartz gets its color from trace amounts of iron, manganese or titanium found within what would otherwise be clear or white quartz. This is another widely abundant mineral that can be found in any magical supply shop, and is often made into pendants, rings, necklaces and other jewelry.

Archeological records dating back to 800 BC show that rose quartz was used in jewelry and cosmetics by the Assyrians, Greeks, and Romans. The ancient Egyptians said that the goddess Isis rubbed rose quartz on her cheeks and around her eyes to preserve her beauty. This skin-care method was a long-held tradition in Egypt, and now that crystals have seen a resurgence in interest over the past several years, it has recently come back into fashion in the West!

The delicate pink color of this crystal makes it a perfect symbol for love and compassion, and it can be used for all magical workings relating to these qualities. Known to many as the Love Stone, rose quartz opens the heart chakra to allow love to penetrate our lives. It aids in healing emotional trauma, resentments, guilt, and anger.

Associated with Venus and the Elements of Earth and Water, rose quartz helps to raise self-esteem and self-worth by reminding us to treat ourselves with gentle forgiveness and kindness, and is a very effective crystal to use during meditation. Indeed, rose quartz enhances one's inner awareness, teaching us that unconditional love is ever present and that we only need to be open to receiving the healing energies of the Universe.

Other magical uses for rose quartz include protection against nightmares and against anger projected by others around you. This is also a popular stone for fertility magic, as well as restoring peace to places disrupted by conflict. In this chapter, you will find rose quartz spells for raising the vibrational frequency of your home, healing and releasing painful emotions, cultivating self-esteem and attracting positive relationships.

HOME-ENERGY TRANSFORMATION SPELL

All homes need fairly regular energetic maintenance in order for the atmosphere to remain ideal. However, when there's been a traumatic or otherwise difficult event—whether involving the home itself or just the inhabitant(s)—it's especially important to address any resulting energetic imbalances. Rose quartz is uniquely suited for this work, as it has the ability to replace negative energy with positive energy.

This spell will help you to clear out and replace any pockets of negative or otherwise unwanted energy in your home. You will be replacing these undesirable energies with the warm, earthy glow of groundedness, peace, and well-being.

Note: This spell is powerful on its own, but for even greater effect, try sweeping and smudging your home with sage before you begin.

You will need:

- 1 medium to large rose quartz crystal per room or area
- White candle (optional)

Instructions:

If using, place the candle at the center of your home and light it.

Spend a few moments quieting your mind.

In each room of your house, find a place to sit in a comfortable position.

Hold the rose quartz between your palms for a few moments, concentrating on the peaceful, positive feeling it emits.

Now place it on the floor in front of you and visualize pink light radiating outward from the crystal, spreading throughout the room.

Feel any negative energy being replaced by a calming, loving vibration from the rose quartz.

When you feel the energy is sufficiently transformed, say the following (or similar) words:

"Love and light are ever present in this space. All is well."

Now pick up the rose quartz and place it in a safe space in the room so that it may continue to balance the energy.

Repeat this ritual in each room or in any area that contains unwanted vibrations.

SPELL TO RELEASE PAIN AND UNEXPRESSED EMOTIONS

Sometimes we are unable to express emotions in certain situations or don't have the words to express our feelings. Stifling our emotions in this way can be a good short-term defense mechanism, but ultimately it will fester and become a source of unattended negativity.

Releasing these painful emotions will enable you to process grief or trauma, heal from emotional wounds, and clear your heart space so that you are open to receive love and compassion from the Universe and from others in your life. This ritual can be used for healing from specific past emotional wounds, or for simply clearing more general emotional clutter from your personal energy field.

You will need:

- 1 rose quartz crystal
- Pink spell candle
- Lavender essential oil (optional)

Instructions:

Light the candle and spend a few moments quieting your mind.

Hold the rose quartz in your left hand. (The left hand allows energy to flow directly to your heart center.) To increase the intensity of the spell, you can hold the rose quartz over your heart.

For three minutes, allow your thoughts to flow naturally, asking for anything that needs to be released to come into your awareness.

Don't hold on to any specific thought—instead, feel it, accept it, and let it move through you. Give the crystal your permission to heal and soothe you by radiating love and understanding throughout your body.

As you breathe, inhale the calming essence of the rose quartz, and on the exhale allow any stuck energy from past pain and trauma to be released.

Anoint the rose quartz with 1 or 2 drops of lavender oil, if using.

Then bury it in the Earth to cleanse it from the energies of the old emotions.

Leave it there for one full night.

You can reuse the stone as often as needed.

ROSE QUARTZ SELF-LOVE AND CONFIDENCE SPELL

In a society focused on materialism and surface appearances, the concepts of "self-love" and "self-confidence" can be confusing. Often people look to their skills and accomplishments for sources of self-acceptance, but this approach is missing the point entirely.

True self-love comes from within, when we recognize that we are divine beings of light no matter how we appear or what we do (or don't do) in the exterior world. This spell is useful for anyone dealing with insecurities or issues of self-acceptance (which is basically everyone, at one point or another!).

If you like, work this spell with a rose quartz necklace or bracelet, for an easily-wearable charm.

<u>You will need:</u>

- 1 rose quartz crystal (or rose quartz necklace / bracelet)
- 1 pink candle
- 1 orange candle

<u>Instructions:</u>

Place the rose quartz between the two candles.

Take a moment to quiet your mind and then light the pink candle, saying the following (or similar) words:

"This light shines as my love for myself shines."

Now light the orange candle, saying the following (or similar) words:

"This light shines as my self-expression shines."

Pick up the rose quartz and hold it between your palms.

Take a moment to focus on the light that shines from the candles, and feel the love emanating from the stone in your hands.

Take a few deep breaths, close your eyes, and repeat the following (or similar) words seven times:

"I accept myself. I trust myself. I love myself. From within, I shine for all the world to see."

Gently extinguish the candles.

Carry (or wear) the rose quartz every day until you feel more rooted in your own confident sense of self.

If you feel the need, you can repeat the spell periodically to recharge the stone (or jewelry).

SPELL FOR ATTRACTING HEALTHY RELATIONSHIPS

The Law of Attraction teaches us that "like attracts like," and that what we think about determines what we bring into our experience. This is true in all areas of life, but is often most clearly seen when it comes to relationships. If you always seem to date the wrong people, or find yourself surrounded by friendships that aren't fulfilling, you need to shift your energetic vibration in order to turn this trend around.

This is easier said than done, however, if you don't have a lot of experience with positive, healthy relationships. Whether you're seeking a romantic partner or a new friend, or both, this spell helps you open yourself up to guidance from the Universe so you can learn to recognize the difference between people who truly value your presence and people who are incapable of treating you well.

You will need:

- 2 small rose quartz crystals
- 1 white or pink candle
- 2 pieces of writing paper
- Fireproof dish

Instructions:

Light the candle and place one rose quartz on either side of it. Take a few moments to quiet your mind.

On the first piece of paper, write down the qualities of friendships and/or romantic relationships that have been unhealthy for you in your life. Don't use names or focus on specific people, but rather strive to articulate the actions that have hurt you and/or the resulting feelings from these encounters. Don't dwell too heavily on any one incident or person, and don't go into more detail than necessary—the point is not to reinforce the negative experiences, but simply to recognize and acknowledge what it is that you wish to be free of in your life.

When you're finished, tear the paper up into a few pieces, and ignite them one at a time on the candle flame, being careful not to burn your fingers.

Drop them into the fireproof dish and let them burn out.

Now use the second piece of paper to write about what you wish to manifest in your future relationship(s). Identify how you want to feel, how you want to be treated, etc. If you're unclear about what healthy relationships are actually like, feel free to write down questions. Let the Universe know what you need in terms of help in shifting these patterns in your life.

When you're finished, fold the paper four times and place it in front of the candle.

Place both crystals on top of the paper and say the following (or similar) words:

"As I value myself, I attract others who do the same
So let it be."

Leave the candle to burn out on its own.

Bury the ashes of the burned paper or scatter them over the Earth.

Keep the folded paper in your journal, Book of Shadows, or somewhere else where you can refer back to it as a "checklist" over the coming weeks and months, as new people make their way into your life.

If you like, carry the crystals with you in a purse or pocket when you go out.

AMETHYST

Another variation of quartz, this gorgeous crystal is found in various shades of purple, from pale lavender to lilac to violet. The color is caused by manganese and iron present in the clear quartz. Many geodes—spherical rocks with crystal-lined hollow cavities—contain amethyst and clear quartz points clustered together. Amethyst is also sometimes found with citrine in the same crystal—this combination is known as ametrine. Amethyst is a fairly abundant mineral, but the largest deposits are found in Mexico, Brazil, Uruguay, Russia, France, and parts of Northern and Southern Africa.

In the ancient world, amethyst was primarily known as a stone that could prevent drunkenness, which we can see in the Greek origins of the name, which translates to "not intoxicate." Both the Greeks and the Romans made drinking goblets encrusted with amethyst, and it is said that the Romans even placed chunks of the crystal into their wine glasses in order to keep from becoming intoxicated. While it's unclear exactly why the ancients attributed this power to amethyst, they must have sensed its high vibrational frequency, as even today this crystal is used in alternative healing to help with recovery from addiction.

Associated with the planet Jupiter and the Element of Air, amethyst has a history of helping bring calm and balance to the emotional, physical, and spiritual realms. It has been used to help people gently work through their grief, tame their emotions, and move past suffering. It can also repel emotional outbursts and dispel confrontational and antagonistic attitudes, making it useful in magical workings related to resolving conflicts of all kinds—even in legal matters. This crystal truly radiates a calming energy, as anyone who wears amethyst or keeps it around the home can attest!

Amethyst is also used in magic for creativity, psychic healing, motivation and protection. It is widely known as an "amplification stone," lending an extra boost to spellwork in general, so it makes a great crystal to keep on your altar at all times! The spells below draw on the energies of amethyst to help you overcome addiction, cultivate patience and flexibility, smooth over legal trouble, and protect yourself from theft while traveling.

RITUAL TO BREAK FREE OF ADDICTION

Amethyst's peaceful, yet highly powerful energies are widely used in spells, rituals and alternative healing modalities to treat addictions of all kinds. This ritual concentrates the properties of amethyst into a protective and supportive talisman for you to keep with you as needed to help you stay out of old, unwanted behaviors.

The "amulet" called for here can be a necklace, bracelet, ring or anklet with at least one amethyst stone in it, but you can also create your own by wrapping an amethyst securely with yarn, twine, or jewelry wire and affixing it to a chain or cord. Many crystal shops also sell necklaces with small wire "baskets" into which any stone can be placed.

Note: if you're struggling with a serious addiction to drugs, alcohol, or disordered eating behavior that poses a danger to your health, please do not rely on this spell alone to solve the problem. Instead, think of it as a powerful step along the path to your recovery, in combination with professional assistance.

You will need:

- 1 amethyst amulet
- Black or violet candle
- 2 pieces of paper
- Fireproof dish

Instructions:

Light the candle and spend some time quieting your mind. When you feel centered, write a list of the negative effects of your habit or addiction on the first piece of paper.

Hold the stone of the amulet between your palms, close your eyes, and take three deep breaths, envisioning yourself free from the effects you've just listed. See your body and mind being infused with bright violet light from the stone, clearing out the old energetic patterns that have held your habit in place.

Now, holding the amethyst in your left hand, use your right hand to ignite the paper on the candle flame. Let it drop into the dish to burn out, as you say the following (or similar) words:

"As I fuse my energy with the power of the divine,
I am freed from this trap; my life is now mine.
So let it be."

Put on your amulet and take three more deep breaths.

Now, on the second piece of paper, write a list of the positive effects that leaving your habit or addiction behind will bring into your life. Allow yourself to feel eager and excited about these benefits of your newfound freedom.

When you're finished, fold the paper three times and place it in front of the candle until the candle has burned all the way down.

Then keep the paper somewhere in your house (or carry it in your pocket or purse) as a reminder of the positive manifestations you are now allowing into your life.

Wear the amethyst amulet (or keep it in your pocket) any time you need energetic support for staying free from your old habit.

BATH SPELL FOR PATIENCE AND FLEXIBILITY

Using crystals in the bath is a great way to create an adjustment in your personal energy field. If you find yourself struggling with irritability and impatience, as we all do from time to time, this ritual bath can help soothe those vibrations and restore you to a sense of peace and acceptance of life's little bumps in the road.

Adding lavender essential oil to the calming energies of amethyst will increase the benefits of this bath, but it's not strictly necessary.

You will need:

- 1 medium to large amethyst
- White or purple candle
- Lavender essential oil (optional)

Instructions:

Light the candle and run the bath.

When the tub is halfway full, add the lavender oil (if using).

Enter the bath and hold the amethyst in your hands under the running water.

Take four deep breaths, inhaling slowly and releasing tension on the exhale.

When the tub is filled, place the amethyst on the floor of the tub near you and sit back and relax.

Stay in the tub for at least 15 minutes.

When you are ready, drain the bath.

Stay in the tub as the water drains, so that any remaining negative energy will be drained away from your body and from the amethyst.

Gently extinguish the candle.

Be sure to cleanse and recharge the amethyst before using it in any other magical working.

SPELL TO RESOLVE LEGAL ISSUES

If you find yourself in legal trouble, whether it's an unpaid parking ticket or something more serious, remaining calm is essential. Amethyst's ability to help resolve conflicts and quell confrontational energies can help you find resolution to your legal matters in a peaceful manner.

To prepare for this working, you might want to try the bath spell above ("Bath Spell for Patience and Flexibility") before you begin.

You will need:

- 1 small amethyst crystal point
- White candle
- 2 small muslin or other fabric squares
- Needle
- Blue thread
- Orange thread

Instructions:

Light the candle and take a few moments to quiet your mind.

Place the amethyst on top of one of the small fabric squares and place the other square on top of it.

Beginning with the orange thread, sew the fabric squares together to enclose the amethyst. As you stitch, reflect as objectively as you can on the circumstances surrounding your legal issue.

Rethread your needle with the blue thread and sew around the edges of the fabric again, this time concentrating your energy on clear communication, truth, and the peaceful resolution of your dispute.

Place the charm in front of burning candle and say the following (or similar) words:

"The powers of truth and reconciliation
now infuse this magical creation."

Allow the candle to burn out on its own.

Put the enclosed amethyst in your pocket or purse when meeting with a judge, officer, or attorney to help you focus your intent and bring about truthful and positive communication.

ANTI-THEFT TRAVEL PROTECTION SPELL

When visiting unfamiliar places, especially crowded cities, it's always wise to keep a close eye on your belongings. You can also use a bit of magic for some extra protection from those who would take advantage of travelers.

This spell uses amethyst to shield you and your belongings from thieves so you can thoroughly enjoy your adventures. You can double or triple this spell as needed so that one charged amethyst is inside each of your travel bags.

You will need:

- 1 amethyst per piece of luggage
- Black spell candle

Instructions:

Light the candle.

Hold the amethyst in your hands and, linking your personal power to that of the Earth, conjure a sense of positive, protective energy.

Focus this feeling into the crystal.

Now visualize the amethyst radiating a purple, protective glow from inside your suitcase (or backpack).

Expand the light so that it infuses all of your personal items, then see it enveloping the entire suitcase.

When you feel the amethyst is fully charged, seal the energy by saying the following (or similar) words:

"I move through this world in peace and safety
with all my belongings secure in my possession.
So let it be."

Place the amethyst in front of the candle until the candle has burned all the way down.

Then place it in your suitcase or backpack during your travels.

You can use the visualization to recharge the amethyst at any point during your journey if it feels necessary.

CITRINE

Another crystal commonly found in magic and gemstone shops, this sunny variety of quartz was named "citron" by the French because of its resemblance to a ripe lemon. Citrine comes in a range of hues from pale yellow to dark amber, fluctuating based on the amount of iron in the quartz crystal.

One traditional nickname for citrine is "the Sun Stone," due to its cheerful color. Many citrines actually sparkle in the sunlight due to flecks inside the stone, and the energy of this crystal is noticeably positive, bringing the essence of sunlight in the form of happiness, contentedness, and joy. In fact, citrine has traditionally been given as gifts to new born babies in order for them to find a lifetime of physical health and emotional confidence.

Citrine was also called "the Merchant's Stone," known to business owners as a lucky talisman to keep in or near the cash register. A unique aspect of citrine's wealth properties is that it not only helps you to acquire wealth, but also to maintain it. While other magical tools call for the creation and accumulation of riches, citrine allows the user to hold on to what they already have so it doesn't slip through their fingers.

Citrine's associations with the planet Mercury and the Element of Air, along with its yellow color, makes it an excellent stone for magic relating to concentration, visualization, decision-making and mental clarity in general. Communication issues and self-expression are also appropriate magical goals when working with this crystal. Anything requiring a banishing of negativity and a boost in positive emotions can benefit from citrine, as this truly is a joyful, uplifting stone.

In this chapter, you'll learn how to use citrine to energetically cleanse your other crystals, improve the quality of your dreams, stay secure in your finances, and rise above fear.

CITRINE STONE-CLEANSING RITUAL

As with all of your magical tools, it's important to keep your crystals and other mineral stones clear of old, unwanted energies. There are many ways to cleanse your stones, but one simple method is to use the purifying, fiery energies of citrine.

For best results, cleanse polished and raw stones separately, as jagged points or edges of raw stones might leave scratches in the polish. And of course, be sure your citrine is energetically clear and charged before using it to cleanse your other stones.

This ritual is best done on a regular basis, perhaps once a month on a sunny day, or on the eve of the Full Moon.

<u>You will need:</u>

- 1 medium to large piece citrine
- Large bowl
- Stones to be cleansed

<u>Instructions:</u>

Place the stones you would like to cleanse in the bowl and place the citrine on top.

Now, focusing on your intention to clear unwanted energy, gently swirl the crystals together clockwise, using both hands.

Repeat this twelve times to cleanse and remove unwanted energies.

When you have completed twelve swirls, remove the crystals from the bowl and return the citrine to your altar.

If you like, you can leave the cleansed stones out in sunlight or moonlight for several hours to charge them with new natural energy.

CITRINE NIGHTMARE-BLASTING SPELL

For anyone who suffers from nightmares, or even just stressful, unpleasant dreams, citrine can work wonders. The bright energy of this crystal is like the Sun bursting through the clouds, restoring color to the previously grey landscape of your sleep. (In fact, you don't have to have "bad" dreams to benefit from citrine—try sleeping with a small piece under your pillow for a few nights and see if you don't notice more pleasant, vivid adventures in your sleep!)

This spell utilizes citrine over the third eye, the spot above and between your seeing eyes that corresponds to your sixth sense. Combining your sixth sense abilities to clear tension from your body with the energies of citrine is an excellent way to improve the quality of your dream experience.

This spell is most effective when worked just before bedtime.

<u>You will need:</u>

- 1 small piece citrine
- Cloth headband

<u>Instructions:</u>

Place the citrine over your third eye and secure it in place with the headband.

Lie on your back and take three deep breaths, focusing only on inhaling and exhaling.

Now, begin an energetic clearing of all tension from your body. Start with your feet, just noticing any tension or stress you carry there. Continue moving up through your body one part at a time – calves, thighs, hips, bowels, stomach, chest, hands, forearms, shoulders, neck, and face. Simply acknowledge any tension you feel in any of these areas—don't worry about them or make any judgements. Be a neutral observer of the energy in your body.

Now visualize a bright, cheerful yellow light moving entering from the soles of your feet. See it traveling up throughout your body, obliterating any tension you discovered during the first part of the clearing process. Take as long as you need to make this visualization effective, and repeat it as many times as you like.

When you feel cleared and relaxed, you can remove the citrine from your third eye and place it under your pillow.

Drift off to sleep, and enjoy better dreams than you've had in ages!

CITRINE CHARM FOR MAINTAINING WEALTH

The ancients of every culture saw the Sun as the source of abundance and prosperity, which could be depended upon to return at the start of each new day. Citrine's association with the Sun makes it an excellent representative of security and long-term abundance.

When you work this simple spell, you reaffirm your appreciation for what you already have, as well as your receptivity to more wealth to come.

You will need:

- 1 small piece citrine
- 1 dollar bill
- Green or black ribbon or thick thread
- Small drawstring bag
- Work candle for atmosphere (optional)

Instructions:

Light the candle, if using. Hold the citrine in your dominant hand and the dollar bill in your other hand.

Take a deep breath and concentrate your energy on merging the yellow light and energy of the citrine with the dollar bill, which symbolizes your current wealth.

Wrap the dollar bill around the citrine.

Now secure the dollar bill with the ribbon or thread, while chanting the following (or similar) words until you have secured it tightly in place:

"I open the path to wealth without end."

Place the wrapped citrine in the drawstring bag and keep it near your safe, checkbook, fireplace, or somewhere else in your home that symbolizes wealth.

SPELL FOR TRANSMUTING FEAR

Most people have to wrestle with fear at one time or another—even Witches with the power of magic at their disposal. Whether you're facing a frightful financial or health calamity, having to conquer a phobia like fear of flying, or worried for someone else you care about, there's a limit to the usefulness of fear.

Fear is basically only good for prompting us to run out of burning buildings or avoid walking alone at night in dangerous places. In other words, fear helps support common sense. Beyond that, however, and especially in circumstances we can't control, fear just gets in the way of clear thinking and empowered decision making. This spell works to transmute the energy of fear from your personal energy field by grounding it into the Earth, restoring you to calm and the ability to trust in the Universe.

Of course, not all fear has an obvious source, and it's not uncommon for people to be living their lives while stunted by a more generalized fearful feeling. This is particularly true for those who are bombarded by advertisements, news stories, and other media that broadcast fearful messages on a daily basis.

If you sense that you're carrying fear around but can't identify the cause, try adding a freewriting session to this spell. You can ask the Universe for help in discovering whether there's something buried in your subconscious, or whether you're simply picking up the fearful energies of the dominant culture at large without realizing it.

This spell is ideally worked with raw citrine, as opposed to polished, so that there's nothing in between the surface of the stone and the Earth when you bury it. However, if you only have polished citrine, don't let that stop you!

<u>You will need:</u>

- 1 piece citrine
- White candle
- Spade or small shovel
- Journal or writing paper (optional)

<u>Instructions:</u>

Light the candle.

If you're incorporating the writing component, spend 10 to 15 minutes writing about the fearful feelings you're intending to transmute. When you've arrived at a satisfactory answer to the question "what am I afraid of?", then you're ready to move on to the next step.

Holding the citrine between your palms, close your eyes and take three deep breaths.

Now, speak your fears into the stone. You can say them as loudly or as quietly as you wish—whatever makes you feel comfortable, but you do need to speak (or whisper) out loud.

Once you have released your fears into the citrine, gently extinguish the candle.

Use the spade or shovel to bury the citrine outside, allowing the Earth to absorb your fear energy and transmute it to neutral energy.

Thank the Earth for participating with you in this work.

For best results, do this step immediately after extinguishing the candle.

MOONSTONE

Moonstone is probably one of the most captivating magical stones in any Witch's collection. This iridescent beauty is often white or cream colored, but can also contain blues, greens, yellows and browns, depending on the specimen. Comprised of two separate minerals, orthoclase and albite, moonstone is a type of feldspar, which is the most abundant mineral group on Earth. The largest deposits of moonstone are found mainly in Sri Lanka and India, but there are many deposits all over the world, ranging from Australia to Brazil to Norway.

Moonstone was highly valued in ancient Rome, where people wore the stone in various forms of jewelry. The Romans believed that moonstone was magically created from solidified moonbeams. Because of this it is strongly linked with the deities of the Moon throughout ancient Rome and Greece. The ancient Egyptians also revered moonstone, associating it with the goddess Isis, and in India it is still considered a sacred stone.

As a member of the feldspar family, moonstone is quite abundant, but the most beautiful specimens are becoming more and more rare due to high demand. Moonstone became hugely popular during the Art Nouveau period, where it was featured in a multitude of jewelry pieces, and men even wore moonstone in their cufflinks and watch chains.

Recently, the mineral has seen a resurgence of popularity in the jewelry world, which may put the most shimmering pieces out of reach for many of the magically inclined. But you don't need to have the most beautiful moonstone in order to work with its potent magical energies!

Not surprisingly, this stone's planetary association is the Moon, with Water as its Element. This makes it a great stone to work with in any spell related to serenity, tranquility, or feminine intuition, as well as any ritual honoring the Goddess. Fertility magic is a natural avenue for using moonstone, as is any working related to women's reproductive health, revitalizing romantic passion, and increasing psychic receptivity.

Traditionally, moonstone was also used for protection while traveling at sea. In this spirit, you'll find a spell below for ensuring safe travel on or over water, as well as spells to support efforts to conceive a child, energize a long-term relationship, and encourage prophetic dreaming.

WATER-TRAVEL PROTECTION CHARM

Travel by sea isn't as common as it was centuries ago, when the tradition of calling on moonstone for safe passage over water would have been widely practiced. Nonetheless, moonstone's watery energy is perfect for a modern-day version of invoking travel protection, whether you're headed to the beach, going on a cruise, flying overseas, or taking a hike along a river.

Mugwort's association with the Moon makes it an ideal protection herb to accompany the moonstone. If you can't find mugwort, however, you can substitute another protection herb, such as valerian or bay leaf.

You will need:

- 3 small moonstones
- 1 teaspoon fresh or dried mugwort
- Small drawstring bag
- Work candle for atmosphere (optional)

Instructions:

Light the candle, if using.

Hold the moonstones between your palms and visualize the beams of the Moon entering each stone. See the white rays of light meeting the stones and charging them with protective energy that will create a magical shield around you on your journey over (or near) water.

Place the charged stones in the drawstring bag, and sprinkle the mugwort over them while saying the following (or similar) words:

"As the Moon casts a glowing path across the sea,
the energies of protection will now surround me."

Close the drawstring bag and leave it under moonlight overnight, either outdoors (ideally) or in a windowsill.

Take it with you on your travels for extra safety.

SPELL TO ENHANCE FERTILITY

Deciding to bring a new soul into the physical plane can be exciting and somewhat stressful on a couple. Many times, conceiving a child does not happen instantly and each passing month may bring about a new level of disappointment. The resulting anxiety can adversely affect fertility.

Moonstone is a powerful magical ally when you are ready to become a parent. This simple but effective spell can soothe any fear about the ability to conceive and therefore enhance fertility. As an added bonus, moonstone is associated with protection of women during pregnancy as well.

You will need:

- 1 small piece moonstone
- Needle and thread
- Tee shirt or other often-worn item of clothing
- Small square of green fabric

Instructions:

Center yourself in the moment by placing the moonstone in your hands and breathing deeply.

Visualize your intent flowing into the stone. See yourself as a parent, welcoming a new life into the world.

When you're ready, turn the shirt or other item of clothing inside out and place the moonstone in a spot that won't get in your way when you wear it.

Place the green square of fabric over it and sew it onto the clothing. As you stitch around the edges, think of the moonstone pouch as a womb for your intentions to conceive a child.

When you have completely encased the stone in the garment, spend a moment holding it in your hands and say the following (or similar) words:

"I welcome you, new child of mine, into this life."

Put on the clothing and wear it for the remaining part of the day.

Leave the stone in your special pouch and wear the clothing often.

Once you've conceived, you can remove the pouch and sew the fabric closed over the stone to make it into a keepsake for your new baby.

MOONSTONE CHARM FOR REKINDLING PASSION

Every relationship needs a boost of renewed zest at one point or another. If you find yourself entering into a less-than-passionate phase with your partner, try working with enchanted jewelry to breathe new life into your current love routine. This working is best performed under the light of a full or waxing moon.

Prices for moonstone necklaces run from affordable to very expensive, but some online research will help you find one that fits within your budget.

<u>You will need:</u>

- 1 moonstone necklace
- Red candle

<u>Instructions:</u>

Light the candle.

Hold the moonstone necklace in your hands and take a moment to remember times when you felt passionate about your partner, and times when your partner demonstrated the same feelings toward you.

Visualize a new encounter with your partner that rekindles these energies.

If there is a single stone in the necklace, concentrate on holding that single stone as you visualize the past and future passion in your relationship. If the necklace has more than one moonstone, repeat the process with each one.

When you have fully charged your necklace with passionate energies, put it on, close your eyes, breathe deeply, and allow yourself to enjoy the anticipation of manifesting your desires on the physical plane.

Gently extinguish the candle.

Wear the necklace on your next date or other quality time with your partner.

MOONSTONE DREAMING SPELL

When we're living fast-paced, hectic lives, our dreams can often seem like just a string of nonsensical "brain garbage" that don't lead to much in the way of insight. But traditionally, dreaming is meant to be a vehicle for important messages from the Universe and our higher selves.

There are many crystals that can help clear out the clutter of our subconscious and smooth out the path for clearer, more profound, and even prophetic dreams to come our way. Moonstone is one of the most powerful dreaming stones, as its energies are linked with the psychic, shifting tides of the Moon.

This spell calls for surrounding yourself with moonstone, creating an energy grid that will help you connect to the ethereal plane in your sleep. You can take it a step further if you like, asking for specific guidance to come to you in your dreams on the night you work the spell.

<u>You will need:</u>

- 4 small moonstones
- Silver candle
- Journal or writing paper

<u>Instructions:</u>

Light the candle and spend a few moments quieting your mind. If you have a specific question or issue that you would like to have addressed in your dreams, write it at the top of a sheet of paper.

Hold the moonstones in your hands and visualize your personal energy infusing them until they glow. Silently ask the stones to harness the energy you need to receive dreams that contain useful information.

Now place one piece of moonstone on the floor at each corner of your bed. As you place each stone, say the following (or similar) words:

"By the light of the Moon, my dreams will flow
and tell me all I need to know.
So let it be."

Gently extinguish the candle before going to sleep.

Keep the journal or writing paper (and pen) near your bed so that you can record your dreams first thing after waking.

CARNELIAN

Carnelian is a variety of chalcedony quartz, colored with reds, oranges, ambers and browns by impurities of iron oxide. Its vibrant colors resemble that of a sunset, which earned it the description "sunset enclosed in stone" in ancient Egypt. Carnelian is relatively abundant and you can likely find it in magical supply shops. Be careful if ordering online, however, as some carnelian stones are actually agates which have been heat treated and dyed.

Found primarily in India but also in South America and Madagascar, this stone has been used for thousands of years to protect against evil energies. It was worn by the ancient Egyptians as a symbol of the goddess Isis to protect against malice, anger and jealousy, as well as for renewal and vitality. Healers during these times used carnelian to help with blood issues. This stone was also part of ancient Eastern burial rituals, often accompanying the dead as a protective talisman.

A stone fittingly associated with the Sun and the Element of Fire, carnelian can be used to enhance one's courage and express one's individuality without aggression. Public speakers, actors and performers of all kinds can benefit from its energy, as suggested by two common nicknames for carnelian: "the Actor's Stone" and "the Singer's Stone."

However, you needn't be a "natural" on stage to benefit from the confidence-granting powers of this stone—anyone finding themselves having to give a presentation or speech can call on carnelian to help them succeed, no matter how much they may fear the task.

Carnelian is a strong ally in protection spells, for as sunlight clears away shadows, this stone's energy banishes negativity. It is also useful in magical workings related to creativity and concentration. It is excellent to use for finding your individuality, your voice, and your own form of expression. Below, you will find spells for protecting against negative energies, encouraging confident self-expression, enhancing creative energy, and sharpening focus and concentration.

EMPATH'S SPELL FOR BANISHING HARMFUL ENERGY

In the grand scheme of things, being an empath is a gift and a blessing, but it can also be a hazard, as ultra-sensitive types can get bogged down, depressed, anxious and even physically ill from overexposure to harmful, lower vibrational energies. Whether it's due to spending all day in a toxic work environment, being the subject of another person's angry or hostile thoughts, or simply being in a physical space where past tragedies have occurred, it's not uncommon for Witches and other magical people to end up being negatively affected by the energy around them.

The bold, grounding power of carnelian makes it an excellent stone of protection against negative influences of all kinds. To boost the overall effect of the spell, try taking a ritual cleansing bath and/or smudging yourself with sage, lavender, or other purifying herbs before you begin.

You will need:

- 1 piece carnelian
- Black candle
- Small bell or chime

Instructions:

Light the black candle and sit in a comfortable chair with your feet flat on the ground.

Holding the carnelian between your palms, take a moment to concentrate on your physical body and set an intention for the clearing of your energy field.

Place the carnelian on the floor at your feet. Starting with the soles of your feet, visualize any negativity surrounding your feet and ankles being absorbed by the carnelian stone. (This energy may take the form of dark, wispy, smoke like-tendrils in your mind's eye.)

Next, place the carnelian in your lap. Visualize it cleansing your calves, thighs, and hip area in the same manner.

Hold the carnelian to your chest to clear the upper torso and repeat the visualization.

Then place it near your throat to cleanse your shoulders and neck area.

Finally, place the carnelian on the top of your head to fully cleanse your whole self and your surrounding aura.

When you're finished, thank the stone and place it in front of the candle.

Ring the bell or chime over the stone to clear and recharge its energy, then gently extinguish the black candle.

Place the stone in a place where you will walk past it multiple times a day, so you can be reminded that you are completely protected from any unwanted energy.

CONFIDENT SPEAKING CHARM FOR INTROVERTS

Many people who are quite articulate in a one-on-one setting find themselves reluctant to speak in group situations, whether it's a college classroom, a meeting at work, or even a social night out. It's not that they don't have anything to say—often they have great insights to share, but just don't quite feel comfortable enough to be the center of the group's attention, no matter how briefly.

If this describes you, try bringing this simple charm with you the next time you're interacting with others. You just might be surprised by the difference it makes!

<u>You will need:</u>

- 1 small piece carnelian
- Yellow, orange or white candle

<u>Instructions:</u>

Light the candle and spend some time quieting your mind.

Think of a recent time when you had something to contribute to a conversation, but kept it to yourself rather than sharing.

Now pick up the carnelian and visualize the scene again, but this time see yourself saying what you wanted to say. See the energy of your statement spreading light like a beacon throughout the atmosphere of the scene. See the other people in the room acknowledging your contribution.

While still holding the stone, repeat the following (or similar) words nine times:

"My voice has value and I am heard by others."

If you like, think of another scene to "rewrite" in this manner, and then repeat the words nine more times. Continue this process until you feel a shift of confidence in your energy.

Carry the carnelian with you next time you are in a group setting and watch as you begin to communicate your thoughts and ideas with confidence.

SPELL TO SPARK CREATIVITY

Whether you're a writer dealing with writer's block, an artist suffering from a lack of new ideas, or just wanting to shake things up a little in any creative area of your life, this ritual is excellent for reconnecting with your individual "muse." It's also great for simply relaxing and transporting yourself out of the daily grind and into playful, magical co-creation with the Universe.

The energy of the carnelian on your paper as you allow your right-brained consciousness to flow makes this crystal a literal "touchstone" connecting you to the higher realms of creative manifestation.

Note: this spell has nothing whatsoever to do with artistic talent, so don't be intimidated if you're not the "artist" type. In fact, if you're someone who is always saying things like "I'm not artistic" or "I'm not really creative," then you should work this spell as often as possible!

<u>You will need:</u>

- 1 piece carnelian
- Orange candle
- White paper
- Markers, crayons, paints, or drawing pencils
- Music (optional)

<u>Instructions:</u>

Light the candle and put on some music that inspires you in some way, if you wish.

Place the paper and drawing/painting implements on the table or altar in front of you. Place the carnelian stone anywhere on the paper.

Now, begin to draw or paint "at random"—don't create a specific image or object. Simply allow your drawing tool to swirl and move across the page freely, without thought or concern for creating a beautiful piece of art. Doodle and dabble and splatter and dot without care. No one will see your creation (unless you want them to).

When you feel that you are done, gently extinguish the candle.

You can place your piece of released creativity on your altar in full view, fold it up and place it somewhere discreet, or even dispose of it if you wish.

Repeat this ritual any time you need to spark a creative burst of energy for a project, or simply want to engage in magical play with the Universe.

SPELL FOR BEGINNING A LONG-TERM PROJECT

Whether you're writing a term paper, putting together a presentation, or even preparing to move house, it can be easy to get lost in the details of a big, multifaceted task. This simple spell helps you stay grounded and focused as you move through the various stages of your project.

The first task for ensuring your ability to focus is to get organized. If you haven't already, take the first few moments of the spell to make a list of the individual tasks that comprise your overall project. For example, if you're writing a paper, you'll need to research, take notes, create an outline, etc. If you're moving, you'll need to make a lot of decisions regarding what to pack first, when to collect boxes, etc. Taking this step will help you reduce any feelings of overwhelm, even before you finish the spell.

You will need:

- 1 piece carnelian
- Orange ribbon or thick thread
- 1 piece of writing paper (optional)
- Several post-it notes or small squares of paper
- Work candle for atmosphere (optional)

Instructions:

Light the candle, if using. Spend some time quieting your mind, and then create the "to do" list discussed above, either on paper or mentally.

Now, write down one task per post-it note, creating a stack of individual, manageable tasks that will add up to the finished project.

Place them in order of what to do first, second, third, etc. (without getting too hung up on individual details, as you want to be able to be flexible while you work). Now stack the notes so that the first task is on top.

Hold the carnelian between your palms, close your eyes, and spend a few moments visualizing the completed project. How will you feel when you're finished? What will the impact of your success be on your daily life? Be as detailed as you can with your visualization.

When you have established a solid, confident feeling about finishing the job, open your eyes and say the following (or similar) words:

"Step by step, one by one,
these tasks of mine will soon be done.
So let it be."

Place the carnelian on top of the stack of notes, and place the stack on your desk or some other place where you will see it often while you work.

As you complete each task, take the corresponding note from the stack under the carnelian and tear it up into pieces.

Enjoy watching the stack grow smaller, and take comfort in the energies of the carnelian helping you to push on to the next step.

BLOODSTONE

Although its common name would seem to imply a predominantly red coloring, bloodstone is actually a deep green form of jasper with flecks of red and brown caused by iron oxide impurities in the stone. The name "bloodstone" comes from Christian mythology, which holds that the blood from the crucifixion of Jesus spattered onto the green jasper stones below the cross. This mineral was also known as "heliotrope" to the ancient Greeks, which translates roughly to "sun stone," as they believed its glinting flecks of color were attracting the light of the Sun.

For thousands of years, bloodstone has been used by various cultures to heal and ground the body through its purification and detoxification properties. The ancient Mésopotamiens dipped the stones in cold water and applied them to the skin over vital organs for detoxification. Bloodstone was also ground to a powder and mixed with honey to draw out snake venom after a bite.

As an all-around promoter of good physical health, bloodstone was believed to be able to stop or reduce bleeding from injuries. Perhaps this is why warriors wore the stone for an extra boost of courage and protection during battle.

Aligned with the planet Mars and the element of Fire, bloodstone supports spells focused around dispelling negativity and can be used to bring positive energy into any situation. Its healing properties make it an excellent stone for work related to physical endurance and stress reduction. It is also used to increase mental clarity and access to one's inner wisdom, helping one to stay in the present moment rather than getting trapped by unproductive worrying. Of course, as a green stone, it can always be added to money spells for an extra boost, and it has also been used in magic related to weather.

The spells below use the properties of bloodstone to help one recognize and avoid deception, strengthen relationships between mothers and children, gain protection from bullies, and make tricky decisions.

BLOODSTONE DECEPTION DETECTOR

This charm is useful in situations where you're not sure you can trust what you're being told, whether it's at work, a social gathering, or even within a relationship. Bloodstone dispels negativity and opens up access to inner guidance, while the color blue is associated with truth, fidelity and sincerity.

As you carry this bloodstone charm with you, it will continue to help you see the truth more clearly.

You will need:

- 1 small piece bloodstone
- Blue spell candle
- Small square of blue fabric
- Blue thread

Instructions:

Light the candle.

Place the bloodstone on top of the blue fabric on your table or altar.

Hold both of your hands above the stone and concentrate on surrounding the stone with the deep blue light of truth.

When you feel that you have filled the stone with your energetic light, repeat the following (or similar) words three times:

"I distinguish between truth and untruth. I am protected from deception."

Wrap the bloodstone carefully in the fabric, secure it with the blue thread, and place it in front of the candle.

Allow the candle to burn out on its own.

Carry the charmed stone with you in your pocket or purse to help protect yourself from deception.

You can also hold it in your hand in your pocket during conversations to feel whether or not you are being deceived.

Recharge it with the above ritual whenever you feel the need.

SPELL TO STRENGTHEN MOTHER-CHILD RELATIONSHIPS

The bond between a mother and her child is sacred and profound, but that does not mean that conflict between the two will not occur occasionally (or quite often!), especially at certain stages in life. This spell helps to strengthen the loving energy between mother and child, and the gift can be given as a means of soothing an existing conflict or preventing a future one.

As a stone sacred to Isis, bloodstone is associated with motherhood, which makes it an excellent focal point for this magical working, but you can substitute another crystal if you wish.

Since this is a gift rather than a charm you use yourself, it's important to be mindful of your intentions here. This working is not about manipulating the thoughts or behaviors of another person, but about fostering a loving energy between two people. The distinction is important, so if you're in a truly hostile conflict with your mother and are unable to summon calm, loving feelings, then this is not a good spell for you to work at this time.

You will need:

- Bloodstone jewelry (such as a ring, bracelet, necklace, etc.)
- Pink candle

Instructions:

Place the bloodstone jewelry on the table or altar in front of you and light the candle.

Hold the jewelry gently between your palms.

Visualize yourself with your mother (or anyone else to whom you wish to strengthen a bond with). See yourself communicating in a calm and peaceful manner. See yourself taking a deep breath when you feel your emotions rising, or politely excusing yourself to be able to take a moment to calm yourself before returning to the conversation.

After the visualization, infuse the necklace with calming energy as you say the following (or similar) words:

"As above, so below
Our relationship continues to grow.
As below, so above
Our communication is filled with love
So let it be."

Give the charmed jewelry as a gift for a birthday or holiday, or as a "just because" present.

ANTI-BULLYING PROTECTION CHARM

Warriors of the past were known to wear a bloodstone amulet close to their hearts in order to give them courage when facing their opponent. The red flecks of fiery Mars energy combined with the deep Earthy green hues imbue a feeling of well-fortified security.

If you're in the unfortunate situation of dealing with someone who behaves in a bullying manner toward you, this protective amulet can shield you from their negativity. Because bullies only target people they think they can have an effect on, you'll soon be well out of their radar and left alone. This is defensive magic at its best!

If you don't have a necklace or pendant featuring bloodstone, you can make one by wrapping wire around the stone and attaching it to any type of necklace cord (see the instructions for "Charm for Intellectual Confidence and Motivation" in the lapis lazuli chapter). You can also find simple cords with small wire "baskets" that allow you to place crystals of your choice inside them, effectively serving as an all-purpose crystal pendant.

<u>You will need:</u>

- 1 bloodstone necklace or pendant
- Black spell candle

<u>Instructions:</u>

Light the candle.

In a sitting position, place the necklace or pendant in your lap.

Begin by visualizing a beautiful green orb at the center of your lap. See the orb gradually grow as it envelops you within it. This is your magical force-field, protecting you against your opponent.

On the outer edge of this shielding energy, visualize vibrant patches of red flaring up to warn away anyone who would do you harm.

When you've summoned a peaceful, protected feeling, hold the bloodstone between your palms and say the following (or similar) words:

"With the Heart of Earth and the Fire of Mars,
I am protected from all who mean me harm
This amulet shields me from their gaze
and sends them on their way.
So let it be."

Place the amulet in front of the candle and allow the candle to burn out on its own.

Then wear it around your neck whenever you may come into contact with those who would bully you.

BIG-DECISION BLOODSTONE DIVINATION

When you're facing a major decision in life with many possible options, it can be hard to get a clear answer from your intuition alone. Bloodstone's Mars-aligned energy makes it a good stone to work with when you need to be pushed a little in the direction that serves your highest good.

During this spell, you will assess all of the possible outcomes of a decision and allow this magical stone to help you decide which course to sail.

You will need:

- 1 small to medium piece bloodstone
- 1 blank, unlined sheet of paper
- Black marker or pen

Instructions:

Take a few deep breaths and reflect quietly on the decision you have before you.

Place the bloodstone in the center of the paper.

With the pen or marker, draw a line radiating outward from the stone for each of your possible options. The lines should be spaced at least an inch apart. (You may want to mark or label each line so you don't lose track of which choice it stands for.)

Now remove the stone and hold it in your hand.

Close your eyes, take a long, deep breath, and then roll or drop the stone in the middle of the paper, taking note of where it lands.

The line it's closest to (or directly on) is the option you're being asked to consider.

Check with your gut—you will get a clear yes or no on this particular choice. Repeat the process as needed until the final choice is clear.

JADE

The stone we commonly refer to as jade is actually two different minerals that have very similar properties. Nephrite and jadeite are physically comparable with their green hues and frequently come intertwined as a single stone. (These two minerals have similar spiritual properties as well, so in magical workings they can be used interchangeably.) Jade has been used in many different cultures for making a variety of items ranging from axe heads to incense burners to jewelry.

Jade is one of the most revered magical stones; its powers have been honored by many cultures from antiquity to the current day. Holding the stone in the palm of their right hands, ancient traders would rely on its powers to make the best decision possible during business transactions. In China, jade has long been believed to harness and hold the power of all five of the Chinese virtues of humanity: benevolence, righteousness, propriety, wisdom, and fidelity. You can find symbols of all five of the virtues carved into jade stones throughout China.

The Aztecs and Mayans also carved images of their deities out of jade and used it for its medicinal properties. Known throughout the world as a stone aligned with the kidneys and bladder, jade has been called by many names, including the spleen stone, piedra de hijada, stone of the loin, yu stone, and the stone of flank. Today, people carry jade in order to support the immune system during times of stress.

Jade is aligned with the planet Neptune and the Element of Water, and its restorative powers provide calming vibrations that envelop the user in a shield of protective energy. Jade promotes balance, wisdom, and peace and is especially useful during unsettling times in life. This stone can help clear out old emotional patterns in order to bring clarity to a confusing situation. Magical uses for jade include protection, abundance, new love, dream work, and gardening. The spells below utilize jade to promote balance and prosperity, help with quick decision making, and resolve feelings of guilt.

A SPELL TO RESTORE BALANCE

Generally when we hear the word "stress," it brings up negative connotations. This is due largely to the imbalances of mainstream modern life, where busyness and noise rule the day, and the importance of connecting with the Earth and the spiritual plane is forgotten. However, stress does have beneficial qualities in moderate amounts, as it helps us recognize when we are overworked, out of balance, or even in danger.

The Chinese symbol of yin and yang represents the balancing of opposites and the interconnectedness of all things. This visual symbol of lightness within dark and darkness within light shows us that the Universe is comprised of seemingly opposite yet complementary qualities, such as forcefulness and patience, firmness and gentleness, and stress and ease.

This spell will help you restore the balance within you, and is useful for times when you feel overly stressed, irritable, or anxious.

You will need:

- 2 pieces of jade
- Yin-yang symbol (drawn or printed)

Instructions:

Place the yin-yang symbol on the altar or table in front of you.

Place one piece of jade on either side of the image.

Spend some time quieting your mind as you hold a soft focus on the symbol.

With your left hand, pick up the jade to the right of the symbol and hold it tight. With your right hand, pick up the jade to the left and hold it equally tight.

Hold one closed palm over the white circle within the black half of the yin-yang, and the other over the black circle within the white half.

Take three deep breaths in this position, and visualize the power of the yin-yang coupled with the energies of the jade balancing any unease in your life. Contemplate any aspects of your life that need more balance and ask the Universe to help you restore equilibrium to those areas.

When you're finished with your contemplation, place the stones directly on the yin-yang symbol.

Leave them on your altar or in another visible place until you feel your balance has been restored.

SPELL FOR PROSPEROUS BEGINNINGS

Whether you're moving into a new home, starting a business, beginning a new job or welcoming a new member into your family, milestones like these are excellent occasions for a little magic.

The scarab beetle was considered a symbol of prosperity and rejuvenation in ancient cultures ranging from Egypt to China. As a magical symbol, it's an appropriate counterpart to jade, which is highly valued as a prosperity stone in the traditional Chinese system of Feng Shui.

<u>You will need:</u>

- 3 small to medium pieces of jade
- Green spell candle
- Potted plant
- Image of a scarab

Instructions:

Place the scarab image on the table or altar in front of you.

Arrange the jade stones in a triangle around the scarab, and place the candle near the top stone.

Light the candle and say the following (or similar) words:

"May luck, fortune and prosperity
accompany me on this new journey."

Allow the candle to burn out on its own.

Bury the jade in the soil around the potted plant (staying clear of the roots) and decorate the pot with the image of the scarab.

Keep the plant in a prominent place where you'll be reminded of its prosperous energy and the exciting potential of the new beginning you are celebrating.

SPELL FOR RESOLVING FEELINGS OF GUILT

Everyone feels guilt over a situation at some point in their lives. Sometimes this is due to choices we've made that caused harm to another, but we may also have feelings of guilt even though we're not at fault. Whether it arises from misplaced blame or actual wrongdoing, lingering guilt is a negative emotion that can sap us of joy, good health, and general well-being.

This spell will help you find the courage to make apologies and reparations if appropriate, or simply allow you to release the guilt and move on with your life. Because you will be burying the jade, unpolished pieces are ideal, but you can still use polished jade if need be.

You will need:

- 1 or more pieces of raw jade

- Light blue spell candle
- Spade
- Journal or writing paper (optional)

Instructions:

Light the candle and spend a few moments contemplating the source(s) of your guilty feelings. You may want to freewrite about it to get to a clearer grip on your role in the situation.

When you're ready, pick up a jade stone and place it on your dominant palm.

Visualize the scenario which has caused you to feel guilt. Close your eyes and allow the jade to soak up this memory.

Now visualize yourself making an apology, if needed, and/ or making any necessary reparations to rectify the situation. Take the healing energy of this envisioned scenario and see it as a white light pouring into the palm of your non-dominant hand.

Place your non-dominant hand over the jade. Allow the feelings of guilt to intermingle with the reparations. Let the jade hold those feelings for you. Depending on the complexity of the situation you are working to heal, you may want to repeat this process with further jade stones.

When the ritual is complete, bury the stone(s) in the Earth to fully release the old feelings of guilt.

If you need to make apologies and/or reparations to others, do so promptly in order to fully heal from the experience.

SPLIT-SECOND DECISION SPELL

We've seen above that bloodstone can help you with the process of making tricky decisions. However, you may not always have the luxury of time to devote to divinatory spellwork to help you reach an answer. As a promoter of wisdom and clarity in fast-moving situations, jade is ideal for situations requiring quick decisions under pressure, whether on the job or in other areas of your life. One charged stone in your pocket or purse can help you make every call with confidence.

<u>You will need:</u>

- 1 medium piece jade

<u>Instructions:</u>

Hold the jade between your palms and take a few deep breaths.

Close your eyes and see yourself enveloped in calm, peaceful energy. In this state you are able to quickly access your inner guidance.

Summon a feeling of confidence and self-trust as you visualize yourself making quick, precise decisions that will have lasting positive effects on those around you.

When you feel ready, send this energy of peaceful self-confidence into the stone, and then say the following (or similar) words:

"As quickly as I touch this stone
all I need for my decision is known.
So let it be."

Carry the jade with you in situations where you encounter the need to make decisions quickly.

LAPIS LAZULI

The enticing blue hues of lapis lazuli have captivated people for millennia. Aptly named from the Latin *lapis* ("stone") and the Persian *lazhuward* ("blue"), this stone is actually comprised of several different minerals: lazurite, calcite, and pyrite, often mixed with other trace minerals. Most lapis stones are a rich medium blue with small gold inflections interspersed throughout. White streaks appearing within the blue are common.

These physical features have linked lapis lazuli to both the day and night sky in many cultures. In ancient Persia, the gold flecks represented the stars, while in medieval Europe the stone represented the blue heavens, and was therefore believed to counteract the spirits of darkness. The deep blue also symbolized royalty and demonstrated their power, honor, and wisdom.

Lapis lazuli was one of the most sought-after stones in history by artists, priests, and members of the nobility. It was inlaid in the sarcophagus of King Tutankhamen. Michelangelo processed it into a fine powder for his many great masterpieces, while Catherine the Great used enormous amounts of the stone to decorate her palace. The most richly colored specimens were used for centuries to make dye, and worn in powdered form as eye-shadow by the ancient nobility.

As a stone associated with the planet Jupiter and the Element of Air, lapis lazuli is linked with truth and knowledge, and Buddhists believe that this magical stone will enable inner peace. Lapis can spark creativity, innovation and motivation while helping to sharpen the intellect through problem solving. Worn at the throat to promote the opening of the throat chakra, lapis allows clear communication to flow through when one speaks.

It has been used in magical work to find truth and honesty, enabling deep communication and self-expression. Other magical uses include enhancing memory, relieving depression, strengthening relationships and enhancing psychic clarity.

In this chapter, you'll find spells to boost your intellectual confidence, help deep communication occur during a difficult conversation, reconnect with the spiritual plane, and showcase your artistic abilities with confidence.

CHARM FOR INTELLECTUAL CONFIDENCE AND MOTIVATION

When you're in the middle of a challenging paper, project, or class, and fatigue sets in, it can be easy to start doubting your ability to complete the work. This charm helps you revitalize your intellectual energy and sharpen your focus on the task at hand.

You will need:

- 1 small to medium piece lapis lazuli
- 4 to 5 inches of thin wire
- 8 to 12 inches of thick thread

Instructions:

Before you begin, take three deep breaths and focus your energy on a white light radiating from your heart center. During each breath, feel the light washing away any negativity or anxiety.

When you're focused and calm, hold the lapis stone in your hands and visualize the paper or project you're working on. See yourself operating from within a flowing current of blue energy as you harness your sharpened mind and successfully complete the work.

Holding on to this feeling of confidence, begin to wrap the wire securely around the stone. See this action as securing your own ability to meet the challenge at hand.

If you like, repeat a mantra such as:

"My mind is sharp, swift, and ready for anything."

Tuck in the end of the wire and then tie the stone to one end of the thread.

Tie a loop in the other end of the thread and hang the pendant on a wall where you work or study.

Whenever you start to falter at your task, look up to the charged stone for renewed confidence and motivation.

LAPIS COMMUNICATION CHARM

Effective communication is essential to healthy relationships. Even when a conversation or discussion will be difficult and potentially painful, it is ultimately necessary to the longevity of a relationship. Lapis lazuli is associated with the throat chakra, the place from which our words flow. Here, you will charge a lapis necklace or pendant with the energies of honest and respectful communication.

If you don't have a necklace or pendant featuring lapis lazuli, you can make one by wrapping wire around the stone and attaching it to any type of necklace cord (see the instructions for "Charm for Intellectual Confidence and Motivation," above). You can also find simple cords with small wire "baskets" that allow you to place crystals of your choice inside them, effectively serving as an all-purpose crystal pendant.

You will need:

- Lapis lazuli necklace or pendant

Instructions:

Place the necklace the table or altar in front of you.

Hold your hands above the lapis lazuli stone(s) with palms facing downward.

Take a moment to focus your intention on the qualities of honesty, wisdom and courage.

When you are ready, send your positive, loving energy into the stone, visualizing the stone and your hands connected by a bright blue light.

After you have charged the stone with your energy for a positive conversation, place the necklace or pendant on your altar until you need to use it.

Wear it during the next difficult and/or deep conversation you have to have in any relationship, to support honest and wise communication between both parties.

GOLD-STAR SPELL FOR A SUCCESSFUL AUDITION

As a stone of self-expression, lapis lazuli is an excellent magical companion for performers of all kinds. The next time you have an audition coming up, try this spell for added confidence and positive energy as you let your talent shine. (Non-performing types can still use this spell for a job interview or even a first date!)

You will need:

- 1 lapis lazuli stone
- Gold candle

Instructions:

Light the candle, and hold the lapis stone between your hands.

Raise the stone so that you can see the gold flecks sparkling in the light of the gold candle.

As you gaze at these "stars," visualize yourself at your audition, confident and full of enthusiasm. See yourself enjoying the experience, and feeling satisfied with your performance at the end.

When you have conjured up a strong feeling of confident enthusiasm, say the following (or similar) words:

"I give thanks for the gold star energy of my success.
So let it be."

Then place the stone on your table or altar and gently extinguish the candle.

Bring the lapis with you to your next audition and keep it on your person throughout, if possible.

SPIRITUAL-PLANE RECONNECTION SPELL

With everything we have to do on the physical plane, day in and day out, it can be easy to run out of time and neglect our connection with the spiritual world. Taking time to reconnect is important because physical and spiritual are interconnected, so to ignore one will inevitably lead to difficulties in the other.

The next time you notice that you've become disconnected from the spiritual plane and don't know how to get "back," try this meditation.

You will need:

- Several (5 to 10) lapis lazuli stones
- Silver candle
- Timer
- Journal or writing paper
- Small cloth bag (optional)

Instructions:

Light the candle and sit in a comfortable place on the floor or in a chair. Make sure that you are able to easily gaze at the light of the candle.

Consciously place the lapis lazuli stones in a circle around you in a clockwise direction.

Set the timer for 7 minutes.

Take a few deep breaths and begin to quiet your mind.

Visualize yourself being surrounded by a protective blue light emanating from the stones. Allow yourself to be receptive to visions, thoughts and other impressions from the spiritual realm by holding a soft focus on the silver candle.

Feel yourself connecting with the spiritual plane and let the images arise as they will until the timer goes off.

Now, write down any images or ideas you received in your journal. You may want to research any images you saw, for further information on what was communicated to you from the spiritual plane.

When you're finished, gently extinguish the candle.

You may want to keep the lapis stones in a small bag to use each time you need to reconnect to the spiritual plane.

MALACHITE

Malachite's deep emerald greens and circular bands of lighter shades create a striking appearance, and its relative softness makes it a popular stone for carving into distinct shapes. This copper carbonite mineral was named by the ancient Greeks after the leaves of the mallow plant (or "malache" in Greek).

Malachite was mined in the Sinai region of Egypt as early as 4000 BCE. Associated with wealth and travel, this was a popular stone with ancient traders and merchants. Traders would wear the stone while conducting business in order to boost the profitability of their transactions. Merchants would keep malachite with their money in order to increase their financial holdings. In many regions, malachite became known as "the salesman's stone." It was also known for its protective properties, however, and was worn in some regions of Italy to ward off the evil eye.

One of the many ways malachite has been used throughout the ages is purification. The intense and healing green of the malachite stone absorbs negativity and pollutants from the body and the environment around us. The toxins of the earth, such as radiation, and the toxins of the body, such as stomach aches, can both be extracted using the magical powers of malachite. Ironically, however, malachite is toxic to the human body and should never be taken in an elixir or ingested in any form. To be on the safe side, work with polished malachite rather than its raw form.

Associated with the planet Venus and the Element of Earth, the protective properties of malachite are quite strong. The stone has been known to break when there is impending danger or splinter to warn of negative energies. Malachite also helps to ward off nightmares and illnesses, and is an especially good protection stone for children.

As a stone of transformation, it is used magically to help change emotional, physical, or spiritual situations from negative to positive by removing the adverse energies. Wearing malachite against the skin helps attract love and make the wearer more ready to let love into their life.

Malachite is used in magical workings related to love, money, travel, protection, and enhancing psychic abilities. It is said that the stone will boost the magical power of spellwork or divination. The spells below utilize malachite to protect sleeping children, reduce road rage, calm fears of flying, and ward off unwanted electronic communications.

ROAD RAGE REDUCTION SPELL

For those who deal with congested commutes to and from work, traffic can really wreak havoc on a positive attitude. Yet those who understand the Law of Attraction know that getting frustrated tends to lead to even more frustrating circumstances!

This fun little spell draws on malachite's ability to neutralize negative situations to help you stay calm, cool and collected in any traffic situation, leaving your ability to attract positive circumstances intact.

You will need:

- 1 small malachite stone
- Small toy car
- Yellow or white spell candle

Instructions:

Place the malachite and the small toy car in the middle of your altar or work space.

Pick up the stone and hold it in your dominant hand.

Close your eyes and visualize yourself in your car on the open road. Allow yourself to feel the ease, joy and freedom of traveling easily and smoothly to your destination.

Take a few deep breaths as you allow this positive vibrational frequency to take hold in your consciousness. Visualize the energy of this feeling infusing the malachite in your hand.

When you feel the stone is sufficiently charged, place the stone on top of the toy car.

Now, visualize yourself stuck in traffic. As you notice the sensations of anxiety and frustration beginning to appear, pick up the malachite and allow the energy you just charged it with to diffuse the negativity you've just conjured. Take note of the difference in how you feel after holding the stone for a few moments.

Place the stone back on top of the car and light the candle as you say the following (or similar) words:

"As the pace of traffic stops and starts
I stay centered in my heart.
No matter how the traffic's flowing
I always get to where I'm going."

Allow the candle to burn out on its own.

Keep the toy car in your glove compartment, and keep the malachite handy to hold onto whenever you end up in congested traffic.

MAGICAL MALACHITE MESSAGE MINIMIZER

Since the advent of the "smart phone," the amount of time we spend dealing with texts, emails and phone calls has more than quadrupled. (For those who also use social media, this distraction factor is multiplied tenfold!) All of this communication can lead to a cluttered mind, making it harder to transition into a magical mindset at the end of the day.

Although the easiest solution is to leave the phone turned off or silence alerts for new messages when we want a break, this isn't always possible. But it is possible to reduce the "noise" associated with unwanted, unnecessary contact with the cyber-world.

Contemporary techno-pagans have found that malachite is useful in protecting against any negative energies associated with our modern forms of communication. Use this spell to help you guard against the minor (or major) interruptions that unwanted emails, texts and/or phone calls can cause in the flow of your daily life.

Note that your intention should be focused on eliminating *unwanted* communication, so that only people you wish to interact with will contact you.

<u>You will need:</u>

- 1 medium to large malachite stone
- Phone (or computer)

<u>Instructions:</u>

Place the malachite on top of your phone or computer.

With your hand still touching the stone, visualize a shield of green light surrounding you and your device, keeping out any unwanted communications.

See the deep green stone soaking up all unwanted, congested energy from your daily interactions on this device and transmuting it into peaceful, quiet energy.

If you like, say the following (or similar) words as you charge the stone with your personal power:

"Do not call, do not press 'send.'
Unwanted messages now will end.
So let it be."

Leave the malachite on or near your device to continue to ward off unwanted communications throughout the day.

ENERGY-PROTECTION CHARM FOR CHILDREN

Children are little psychic sponges, and are constantly picking up on the moods and emotions of adults, whether we realize it or not. Some children are far more sensitive than others (especially those who end up interested in the magical arts!) but all youngsters are energetically vulnerable to their surroundings to some degree.

Even the most loving parents go through emotional struggles which can seep into the subconsciousness of their children. This is all part of human development, but we can use magic to minimize the effects our own negative energies have on the young people around us.

Malachite is traditionally known as a protection stone for children. Making a malachite charm to hang in your child's room creates an invisible shield to keep out unwanted energies, entities, and anything else on the ethereal plane that might cause unnecessary difficulties.

It's ideal to hang this charm in a window so that it can charge daily in the sunlight. If this isn't possible, just be sure to charge the stone regularly—preferably in direct sunlight.

<u>You will need:</u>

- 1 small to medium piece malachite
- 4 to 5 inches of thin wire
- 8 to 12 inches of thick thread
- Hook
- Work candle for atmosphere (optional)

<u>Instructions:</u>

Light the candle, if using.

Spend some time quieting your mind and breathing deeply. This is a particularly important first step, given the focus of this working—you don't want any stress, worry, or other negative energy to be in your field as you create and charge this charm.

Hold one end of the wire against the malachite and begin to wrap the length of it around the stone.

As you work, visualize the stone radiating positive energy throughout the child's room and continuing on out through the window. See the energy of the stone breaking through and dissipating any harmful energy that could enter your child's unconscious mind.

As an extra energetic boost, try singing or humming a lullaby while you secure the stone within the wire.

Use the thread to create a hanger for the stone with a loop.

Place the hook above the window and hang the pendant in the sunlight (if possible), being careful to hang it high enough to be out of the reach of children.

SPELL TO SOOTHE FEARS OF FLYING

Even in this modern age of frequent air travel, fear of flying is not uncommon. If this phobia has kept you on the ground in the past, try harnessing the protective, calming energies of malachite to help you overcome your fear.

This spell involves calling on the protective powers of a chosen deity or other magical being. If you work with the God and/or Goddess, you can call on them directly for this spell, or find an aspect of them among the ancient deities associated with journeys, such as Hermes, Apollo or Rhiannon. Alternatively, you could ask for the assistance of Archangel Raphael, who guards travelers. If you work with the Elementals, then call on the sylphs to keep you uplifted and feeling safe during your flight.

You will need:

- 2 small to medium malachite stones
- Sheet of white paper

Instructions:

Take three deep breaths and visualize a white light radiating from your center. Allow the light to grow on each inhale until you are fully enveloped in a soft white glow.

When you're ready to begin, use the white paper to make a paper airplane. You can fold you plane in any design that you like.

Place one malachite stone on each of the wings. Focus your energy and intent on the plane as you let it represent your upcoming travel.

Now visualize yourself being carried on the wings of your chosen magical helper(s). Imagine them transporting you gently through the sky, knowing that on their wings you are safe and can relax.

Spend a few moments holding fast to this vision, and then place the stones on your altar until your next journey through the air. You can keep the paper airplane on the altar as well, or recycle it.

Bring the charmed malachite with you in your pocket or purse for your next flight.

During takeoff (and throughout the flight if need be), hold the stones to recall the safe and relaxing feeling you had during your visualization. Silently ask your chosen magical helper(s) to stick close to you throughout the flight.

TIGER'S EYE

Tiger's Eye is a macrocrystalline quartz comprised of multiple interwoven layers of earthy browns and glimmering gold hues. The resemblance of the stones to a tiger's fur as well as the appearance of "eyes" in many of the polished stones led to the name of this mineral. As animal symbols, tigers represent power, elegance, and strength, and these characteristics are associated with the stone as well.

The ancient Egyptians used tiger's eye stones as actual eyes in sculptures of their gods and goddesses, representing the ability of the divine to see all and know all. In the East, tiger's eye has long been associated with good fortune and wealth. Ancient Roman soldiers wore and carried the stones in battle, as they believed it had the power to make weapons bounce off of their armor. More significantly, these amulets gave the wearer courage to stand up to an enemy on the battle field and fight for what he believed was right.

Tiger's eye is useful for focusing the mind, bringing about clarity, enhancing spiritual visions, and supporting the necessary change that must occur during the journey of life. The magical powers of this stone grant the user courage, integrity, and the ability to use one's power for the good of the physical and spiritual realms. Associated with the Sun and the Elements of Earth and Fire, this stone is also used in workings for protection from psychic attack, wealth and prosperity, and good fortune in new ventures. As a grounding stone, it is useful for "earthing" after magical rituals.

Some people utilize tiger's eye's animal association to work magic for the protection and conservation of tigers and other big cats, both in the wild and in refuge parks. In this chapter, you'll find spells using tiger's eye to bring prosperity to a new business venture, seek clarity in a murky situation, and provide yourself with a boost of courage and bravery, along with a creative divination ritual.

SPELL FOR A SUCCESSFUL NEW BUSINESS

Starting a new business is an enormous leap of faith, even for the most experienced entrepreneurs. This spell helps you get off on the right foot, joining an object of personal significance to you with three chief properties of tiger's eye: wealth, prosperity and good fortune. You'll be creating a talisman to visually remind you of your upcoming success throughout each day.

You will need:

- Several small tiger's eye stones
- Green or gold candle
- Journal or writing paper
- Small bowl, dish, or cup that has personal significance

Instructions:

Light the candle and take a few deep breaths.

Spend some time thinking about what "success" in your business looks like. Perhaps it's a store full of customers browsing the merchandise, or a large staff of well-compensated employees. You might envision several five-star reviews on a social media website, or satisfied clients referring your business to their friends.

Do some brainstorming along these lines and make a list of as many different manifestations of "success" as you can think of. Be as specific as you can with the details.

Now hold one of the tiger's eye stones in your hand and make a loose fist.

Close your eyes and visualize one of the manifestations from your list, being as rich in detail as you can.

Place the stone in the bowl, dish or cup.

Repeat this process with the rest of the stones—visualizing your success and then placing the energy of it into the vessel.

When you are done, find a special area in your new business to place the vessel in order to ensure good fortune and success.

REFOCUSING SPELL FOR LONG-TERM PROJECTS

When working on long-term projects such as academic papers or presentations, it's easy to get bogged down in the nitty-gritty details and lose focus, which makes it hard to stay motivated. Even when taking a practical approach, such as starting with the easiest aspects and saving the hardest parts for later, there are moments of overwhelm that can make finishing the work seem impossible.

In this spell, tiger's eye represents the "all-seeing eye" that can view every angle of a situation. You will draw on its energies to rise above the details and see the project come together into a cohesive whole. The colors blue and yellow are associated with the Element of Air, which rules the intellect. Yellow is specifically associated with concentration and writing, while blue embodies the qualities of peace, patience, and wisdom.

You will need:

- 1 medium to large tiger's eye stone
- 1 sheet of standard size yellow or blue paper
- Several small slips of paper

Instructions:

Place the tiger's eye in the center of the blue or yellow paper on your altar or work space.

On each of the slips of paper, write a word or phrase that represents an angle of the project that you're struggling with. These can be larger issues, such as meeting the project deadline, down to the smallest, most confounding details, such as how to rework a disorganized paragraph.

Once you've written each issue on a slip of paper, take a moment to focus your gaze on the tiger's eye. Visualize yourself looking at the project from a high vantage point and see it coming together as if being sewn with gold stitches by an unseen hand.

Hold this vision for a few moments and allow a feeling of confidence to build within you. When you feel sufficiently confident about finishing the project, collect all the slips of paper and fold them into the blue or yellow paper.

Place the tiger's eye on top of the folded paper and leave it on your table or altar until you have completed the project.

TIGER'S EYE COURAGE SPELL

Tiger's eye empowered even the strongest Roman soldiers to be brave and courageous during a battle. Just as these soldiers used tiger's eye to deflect weapons wielded by those attacking them, we can use tiger's eye to deflect fear caused by challenging social situations.

This spell will enable to you to create a metaphorical shield to bring with you into whatever battles you face, be they dealing with intimidating coworkers, a difficult conversation with your boss, or even a holiday dinner with your in-laws.

You will need:

- 4 pieces of tiger's eye
- Red spell candle
- Small cloth bag

Instructions:

Take a few deep breaths and center yourself.

Visualize the upcoming encounter you're concerned about. See yourself in the moment after the encounter has come to a close, feeling relieved and satisfied with your handling of the situation. You don't need to envision any of the details—simply focus on the *feeling* of having successfully navigated the challenge.

When you're ready, light the candle. Place the first stone in front of the candle and say the following (or similar) words:

"I honor myself for acknowledging my fears."

Place the second stone behind the candle, directly in line with the first, and say the following (or similar) words:

"I trust my intuition to guide my words."

Place the third stone to the right of the candle and say the following (or similar) words:

"I affirm my ability to communicate with integrity."

Place the final stone to the left of the candle, directly in line with the third, and say the following (or similar) words:

"I stand in my sovereignty no matter the actions of others."

Allow the candle to burn all the way down.

Gather the stones into the bag and keep it with you during the upcoming encounter.

Visualize the stones creating a protective shield around you as you navigate the conversation(s).

SCRYING WITH TIGER'S EYE

Tiger's eye is associated with both the Sun and the Earth, which makes perfect sense given its interwoven layers of gold and brown. As such, this stone is also a promoter of energetic interaction between the physical and spiritual planes.

This divination method utilizes the shimmering exterior of polished tiger's eye stones, along with water and sunlight, to facilitate striking visual images that can communicate messages to the receptive practitioner. It is best performed outside on a sunny day, but if this isn't possible, a sunny window can also work.

<u>You will need:</u>

- Several (10 to 20) small to medium tiger's eye stones
- Glass dish
- Cup of water
- Sunshine
- Journal or writing paper

<u>Instructions:</u>

Place the tiger's eye stones in the glass dish.

Pour the water over the stones until the dish is nearly full (but don't allow it to spill over the edge).

Take a few deep breaths and clear your mind.

Keeping your focus soft, gaze on the small pool of water and the reflections of the stones. Be open to any images or visions that arise.

When you have finished, record your images and thoughts in your journal to further explore.

JET

Unlike the other crystals and stones featured in this collection, jet is actually a fossilized wood rather than a true stone. As the araucaria trees of the Jurassic period began to die off, their decaying wood ended up in swamps, rivers, and other bodies of water. The wood was eventually flattened by the pressure of multiple layers of organisms and mud over millions of years. Chemical changes ultimately morphed the remnants of this once grand tree into gleaming black stones.

Named for a region in Asia Minor, the color of this stone is the source of the phrase "jet black," used to describe anything that is as black as it is possible to be. However, some specimens may actually be browner in color.

Jet has been used since prehistoric times—it has been found in burial mounds as far back as 1400 BCE—and was prized for its protective properties by ancient travelers and soldiers alike. Although it is a soft, dull stone in raw form, jet can withstand a high amount of polishing, which enables it to take on a mirror finish. In fact, it was often used for this purpose during medieval times.

It was also widely believed in many cultures during this period that inhaling the smoke from burning jet was physically and spiritually beneficial. In more recent history, jet became well-known as a "grieving stone" after Queen Victoria of England wore it while mourning the death of her husband, Prince Albert.

Like many black stones, jet removes unwanted energetic attachments and absorbs negativity. It's a great stone for meditation and for healing grief. Associated with the planet Saturn and the Element of Earth, jet is used in magical workings related to purification, psychic protection and increased psychic awareness, promoting luck related to money, and divination. Like malachite, it is known to increase the effectiveness of magic when placed on the altar or other work space.

The workings below show you how to use jet to create a pendant to ward off nightmares, to cleanse your aura, to support yourself during a time of grief, and to promote success at a new job.

ANTI-NIGHTMARE PROTECTION CHARM

Jet is a great stone to use in sleep magic, especially for those who suffer from nightmares or other sleep disturbances.

Jet beads can be found through crystal and mineral retailers and at craft stores (though be sure to double check at craft stores that you're not getting imitation glass beads). If nothing else, you can buy a jet necklace or bracelet and unstring it in order to create this sleeping charm from scratch.

You will need:

- 10 to 15 jet beads
- Several inches of thick silver thread
- Scissors
- Thumb-tack or hook
- Work candle for atmosphere (optional)

Instructions:

Light the candle, if using.

Spend some time taking deep breaths and quieting your mind.

When you're ready, begin by cutting a long piece of silver thread.

Tie a knot at the end of the thread, making it large enough that the jet bead will not slip off.

Place one bead on the thread and say the following (or similar) words:

"Peaceful sleep I shall find,
all my nightmares I now bind."

Tie a knot and then repeat the chant as you place the next bead on the thread.

Repeat this process until all the beads have been strung.

Use the scissors to cut the thread, leaving enough to tie a small loop.

Use the loop to hang the pendant on a tack or hook above your bed.

AURA PURIFICATION RITUAL

Everyone has an aura—the subtle energy field that surrounds us and extends outward from our physical form. Our thoughts, actions, diet, and physical environment have an effect on our aura, so that it changes depending on how we're feeling and thinking, and how we're treating our minds and bodies. Those who can see auras are able to tell if a person's overall energetic state is healthy or in need of assistance, based on the vibrancy (or lack thereof) of the colors swirling in their auric field.

You don't need to be able to see your own aura, however, to know if you're energetically "down in the dumps." This spell uses the purifying properties of jet to cleanse troublesome, murky, or stagnant energies in your personal auric field. Use it in conjunction with healthy food, exercise, and regular meditation (or other spiritual activity) to keep your aura vibrant and colorful.

<u>You will need:</u>

- Several (10 to 30) pieces of jet
- Pillows
- Small cloth bag (optional)
- Work candle for atmosphere (optional)

<u>Instructions:</u>

Light the candle, if using.

Take three deep breaths and release any little disturbances from your day on each exhalation.

Lie down in a comfortable place on your floor, using pillows to support yourself so that you are able to fully relax.

Place the jet stones around the perimeter of your body, paying mindful attention to each placement.

Now take a few more deep breaths and begin to activate your third eye, or "second sight."

Starting with your feet, mentally scan each part of your body. As you move slowly up your body, be aware of any part that feels stuck, dark, or otherwise less-than-optimal in terms of energy. Don't over analyze this—rather, let your intuition guide you.

Visualize a white light over any area you feel is energetically weakened or out of balance, in order to send power and energy back to that spot.

When you have completed a full scan of your body—feet, calves, knees, thighs, groin, intestines, stomach, chest, neck, arms, hands, and head—visualize your entire body full of white light.

Continue to lie there and relax fully for 10 to 15 minutes.

You may want to keep the jet stones in a small bag to use each time you need to cleanse your aura.

Be sure to cleanse the stones in between uses, by smudging them with sage or smoke from a purification incense.

RITUAL FOR EASING GRIEF

When someone you're close to passes on to the next world, it's important to allow yourself to grieve. Grieving is a natural and healthy reaction to loss. But grief is a process, and eventually it is necessary to let go of grief and move forward with our lives. If you find that after much time has passed you are not making progress in this regard, a ritual of memorial can help.

Jet's ability to assist with purification of unwanted energies makes it an appropriate stone in this situation. Furthermore, jet facilitates increased psychic awareness, which can help you sense when your loved one is near, provided you are open to it.

In this ritual, you will be celebrating positive memories of your loved one. You will also be speaking of these memories aloud, as giving voice to your experiences with this person will help you release sadness that has ceased to serve its purpose. If you are open to it, you may sense that your loved one is listening, and lovingly appreciating your honoring of them in the physical world.

You will need:

- Several (10 to 20) jet beads
- Necklace cord with clasp or thick thread
- White candle

Instructions:

Light the candle and take three deep breaths.

Holding a jet bead in one hand and the necklace cord or thread in the other, recall a positive memory of the person you are grieving. This can be a particular story, a character trait you admired in the person, or something joyful about your relationship with them.

Speak out loud about this memory. If you feel inclined, speak to the person. Or you can speak about them. For example, you can say "You always asked me how my day went when I came home," or "She had the best laugh."

After speaking of the memory out loud, string the bead onto the cord or thread.

Repeat this process for each of the jet beads.

When you have finished, secure the clasp or tie a knot in the thread.

You may wish to wear the beads as a necklace, place them on your altar, or hang them in a special place in your home.

At some point in the future, you may feel that it's time to let go of the string of beads or store them in a place where you won't see them. This is fine, and should be taken as a sign that you have moved forward significantly in your grieving process.

JET GIFTING SPELL

When it comes to working magic for others, there are ethical concerns to be aware of. Because each person's path in life is truly their own, it's not up to us to cast spells for others without their permission, no matter how benevolent our intentions are. If you are asked to work a spell for someone else, then by all means do so. But what if you're wanting to give a magical gift to someone who wouldn't understand or believe in magic?

This spell is a good example of how you can share your magical talents with others without being unwittingly manipulative or needing their permission. It can be done with any stone for any purpose, but here we will work with a specific tradition—giving jet to a person who has just landed a new job.

Jet is a powerful beacon of good luck, supportive energies, and personal calmness as well as stability under pressure. It is considered the perfect gemstone to give to someone special to honor their beginning in a new job.

This simple act is a wonderful way to use your positivity and magical skills to honor and celebrate a friend's or other loved one's achievement. You can tell them that jet is a traditional good luck stone for those who are starting new jobs. Whether or not you tell them that you charged it with your own positive energy is up to you.

You will need:

- Jet stone or piece of jewelry featuring jet
- Small jewelry box

Instructions:

Place the jet stone or piece of jewelry on the altar or table in front of you.

Take a few minutes to focus on the recipient, noting the positive aspects of their character and the skills they will bring to their new position. Visualize them in their new job being successful and content.

Concentrate your positive vibrations into the object by placing your hands above the jet.

When you have fully imbued the stone with your encouraging and optimistic energy, place it in a small box.

Give the gift to your friend or loved one and know that each time they wear the jewelry or place the stone in a space at their new position, they will be filled with the good wishes you have intended for them.

HEMATITE

One of the most common minerals on Earth, hematite is found in countries as far apart as Brazil, Norway, Italy, and Canada. This stone's outer appearance is a silvery-grey color that polishes to an immaculate shine, giving it the appearance of steel. Its inner core, however, is a blood red color derived from the iron oxide in its mineral composition. In its pure form, hematite can often develop into structures that appear to have petals like a flower. These forms are called iron roses.

The name hematite comes from the Greek word *haimatites* which roughly translates to "blood," due to its ochre interior. In fact, for many centuries, hematite was called "bloodstone," though we now use that name for the green jasper featured earlier in this book. At least one myth about the stone's origins was related to battle—as soldiers lay injured in the aftermath of a fight, large pools of blood would accumulate and sink into the earth, forming the mineral.

Hematite's smooth, glasslike surface made it a perfect crystal for using as a rudimentary mirror in ancient times. The powdered interior was used as a pigment in some cave paintings, and by the ancient Egyptians who painted their pharaoh's tombs and sarcophaguses to depict images of the afterlife. Native Americans also used hematite to paint their faces before going into battle.

Despite its many associations with blood and battle, hematite is also known as a stone linked to the higher mind. It helps to center and organize energy by grounding and calming the user. The ability to focus while experiencing multiple stimuli simultaneously can help to reduce stress and anxiety in social situations. Associated with Mars and Saturn, and the Elements of Fire, Earth, and Water, hematite is used in magical workings related to grounding, psychic awareness, healing, past life recall, logical and critical thinking, self-esteem and confidence, and dissipating negative energy in one's surroundings.

The spells in this chapter utilize hematite to help you release worry and anger, transform pessimism into optimism, and ground yourself during social interactions that may cause heightened anxiety.

SPELL TO BOOST OPTIMISM

Anyone who understands the Law of Attraction knows that our thoughts create our reality. Therefore, keeping an upbeat and optimistic attitude is crucial to our ability to manifest what we desire. This is easier said than done, however, and even the most positive people occasionally find themselves slipping into pessimistic thinking. Hematite's grounding and healing properties can be harnessed to help you turn your attitude around, and go back to attracting positive thoughts and experiences.

The hematite in this spell works on two levels. First, it assists you in reprogramming your negative thoughts into positive statements. It also wards off any other general negative energy that you may have been unwittingly attracting during your bout with pessimistic thinking.

Although you may be able to identify a multitude of negative thoughts, it's best to just work with a small handful, in order to focus your intention on the act of transmuting the negative into positive. Otherwise, you may get overwhelmed or your focus may dissipate through the effort of rewriting too many separate thoughts. So just focus on the main issues that have been coming up for you repeatedly.

<u>You will need:</u>

- 3 to 5 hematite stones
- 3 to 5 small slips of paper
- White candle

<u>Instructions:</u>

Light the candle and spend some time quieting your mind.

When you're ready to begin, recall a particular negative thought that you have been having recently.

On one of the slips of paper, rewrite the negative thought into a positive statement. For example, if you keep thinking "I never have any money," you can write "I believe money can flow to me without having to know its source."

Wrap the slip of paper around the hematite stone so that the words are facing outward.

Secure the paper with a drop of wax.

Repeat this process with the remaining hematite and paper.

Leave the paper-wrapped stones on your altar or place them in an area where you spend a lot of time, to help you remember to transform your negative thoughts into positive statements.

When your pessimistic "funk" has lifted, thank the stones and recycle the slips of paper.

SPELL TO EASE SOCIAL ANXIETY

Those who suffer from social anxiety know that it doesn't only occur in large group situations. Depending on your level of sensitivity to other peoples' energy, anxiety can crop up during all kinds of encounters with other people.

In this spell, you will create a helpful talisman to carry in your pocket, helping you to remember to ground and center yourself during social interactions.

<u>You will need:</u>

- 1 medium hematite stone
- White or black spell candle

Instructions:

Light the candle and spend some time breathing deeply to quiet your mind.

When you feel ready, spend a few moments visualizing the kind of social situation that makes you uneasy.

Ask yourself what triggers an anxiety producing response in your body during these situations.

When you identify a trigger, pick up the hematite and hold it between your palms.

Take a deep breath and exhale slowly, counting to seven.

Envision yourself in this imagined social setting, surrounded by white light.

Repeat this breathing process three times, focusing on filling the stone with tranquil, relaxed energy.

Now, place the hematite in front of the candle.

Allow it to charge there until the candle has burned all the way down.

Carry the charmed stone with you in your purse or pocket the next time you are entering into a social situation that may produce an anxious reaction. You can hold on to the stone during any difficult moments without anyone even knowing!

ANGER-RELEASE SPELL

Anger is a normal human emotion that has its place, temporarily, in certain situations. However, it's best for your health—mental, physical and spiritual—to release anger once it has served its purpose. This spell will help you remove the energy of lingering resentments and move on so that you can experience positive emotions, like joy, love and hope, more fully and clearly.

Hematite's healing properties and its ability to dissipate negativity makes it a great stone for this kind of work. The Earth's power to transmute negative energy into neutral or positive energy is also utilized in this spell. Raw hematite is best for burying, but a polished stone will also work in a pinch.

<u>You will need:</u>

- Small to medium raw hematite stone
- Black or white candle
- Journal or writing paper (optional)

<u>Instructions:</u>

Light the candle, and spend some time quieting your mind.

Allow yourself to focus on the anger and/or resentment you're still carrying with you from an old situation.

If it helps, do some freewriting about the issue—try to identify the reasons for the anger you're still feeling.

When you're ready, hold the hematite between your palms.

Visualize the feelings you're looking to release flowing into the stone, making it grow warm and heavier in your hands.

Go outside and bury the stone in the Earth.

As you dig the small hole and cover the stone, say the following (or similar) words:

"Let this pent-up anger cease.
These old feelings I now release.
Blessed Be."

SPELL TO RELEASE THE HABIT OF WORRY

Planning ahead is a valuable skill to have in life, but constantly worrying about what may or may not happen is actually counterproductive to manifesting the reality you desire. If you're a chronic worrier, you're certainly not alone.

However, you can empower yourself to ditch this habit with the help of the powers of Nature. The soothing effect of running water in this spell combines with the transmuting power of hematite to help you release your habit of worrying and clear up your energy field for a smoother, more carefree life.

If you don't live near a stream or creek, you can place the stones in a bowl and run water from the sink or bathtub over them for several minutes and then scatter the stones over the Earth. However, it's highly recommended that you make the effort to bring them to a natural body of water, even if you have to go out of your way to get there.

<u>You will need:</u>

- Several raw hematite stones
- Small cloth bag

<u>Instructions:</u>

Spend some time quieting your mind.

When you feel ready, take one stone and hold it between your palms.

Think of a specific worry that you are currently experiencing and let the hematite absorb the worry.

Place it in the small bag.

Continue this process with as many stones as you need.

Bring the bag of hematite to a nearby stream, river, or creek.

Sit quietly for a few moments at the edge and allow the sound and sight of the moving water to soothe your spirit.

When you feel ready, gently empty the bag of stones into the running water.

Thank the Elemental spirits of the water for cleansing your energy of worry and fear.

The next time you find yourself starting to anticipate something negative happening in the future, return in your mind to the water running over the hematite stones.

If you can, get into the habit of listening to recordings of a bubbling brook, a waterfall, or even the ocean in order to help you maintain a calmer state of mind.

CONCLUSION

Crystals are the most delightful magical companions. Their mere presence creates a special ambience wherever they are found. This is especially true when they are well-cared for and frequently utilized, so be sure to acknowledge and appreciate any crystals and stones that come into your life.

However, don't feel that you need to acquire a large collection of crystals in order to make the most of the opportunities they present. A modest handful of your favorite stones can be far more powerful than an overwhelming array of them cluttering up your altar.

Don't feel that you need to keep every single stone you encounter for the rest of your life, either. As you become more receptive to communication these magical beings offer, you will sense when a stone is ready to "move on" from the relationship. When this happens, you can give it as a gift or leave it as a surprise somewhere for someone else to come across. When it comes to raw stones, you can also simply return them to the Earth.

So take your time acquiring and learning to work with crystals. After all, these beautiful stones have been on the Earth for millions and even billions of years! They will be infinitely patient with you as you grow in your practice, so be patient with yourself as well. Enjoy following your path with crystal magic, and Blessed Be!

WICCA

BOOK OF HERBAL SPELLS

A Beginner's Book of Shadows for Wiccans, Witches, and Other Practitioners of Herbal Magic

LISA CHAMBERLAIN

CONTENTS

INTRODUCTION

Welcome to my *Book of Herbal Spells*! Herbal magic is a wonderful form of magic to practice, as it keeps Witches literally in touch with the powers of the Earth—not to mention the Sun, the rain, and the wind!

This collection of spells, rituals, and other workings is devoted to the magical energies of the plant kingdom, and can be used on its own, or as a companion to *Herbal Magic*. Each spell is relatively simple and suitable for beginners to magic, yet can inspire more seasoned practitioners as well.

Complex spells with multiple ingredients can be very enjoyable and certainly serve a purpose. However, I find that zeroing on one or two ingredients can really hone my focus, and help me get better acquainted with herbs that are new to me.

In that spirit, single herbs are often the focus of these spells, with minimal additional ingredients, in order to help you deepen your own magical relationships with these powerful herbs. In fact, the spells are even organized by herb, rather than by purpose or form, in order to give you an opportunity to work closely with individual herbs, one at a time.

For readers of *Herbal Magic*, all 13 herbs will be familiar, though some new information about each is featured here, in addition to the new spells. Other readers, depending on experience level, may be acquainted with some of these herbs, while other ones might be new.

Most of these herbs can actually be found in the spice section of any grocery store. Only a few—elecampane, mugwort, hibiscus and dandelion—might require a bit more searching, but they can definitely be found in natural food stores and cooperatives, as well as at metaphysical stores and online.

For people new to magic, a few practical tips are worth reiterating here. First, please note that the instructions for each spell assume that you have already charged your ingredients for the magical purpose you are working for.

Methods for charging tend to vary according to what it is you're working with, but if you're not sure how to proceed, you can use a standard method that works for most anything: lay the herb or other object on an already-charged pentacle, and speak words of intention related to the spellwork you'll be doing.

Depending on your practice, you might invoke the Goddess and God, the Elements, or other spiritual energies you work with. If you haven't yet learned to charge ingredients, research and try a few different methods for charging various tools, until you find what feels most appropriate for you.

Second, know that the amounts and proportions listed for each spell are general suggestions—there's no need to measure out *exact* teaspoons or tablespoons, unless you find that doing so adds energy and focus to the spell. Otherwise, a rough estimation of the listed amount will do—as always, go with your gut instinct!

As for candles, which appear often in these pages, some spells include instructions for what to do with the candle when the spell is over, while others do not. If it's left unspecified, you can choose to leave the candle burning or snuff it out gently (with a candle snuffer or by waving your hand). You can use the candle again for atmospheric lighting, or for repeats of the same spell, but avoid reusing candles for different spells altogether.

Finally, always remember that no matter the quality of your ingredients, how well you charge them, or how well you follow the spell instructions to the letter, your state of mind is the chief factor in any successful spellwork. Approach a spell with doubt that it will work, and you've pretty much guaranteed that it won't! Approach it with anxiety, and you're likely to get mixed results or no results at all.

The most successful magic is done from a place of calm centeredness and with very focused intent. So always do whatever you need to do to get grounded, whether that's through meditation, visualization, breathing techniques, a ritual circle-casting, or all of the above.

Many of these spells include reminders to spend time quieting your mind, but it's up to you to take this step. It is ultimately *your* energy that's shifting the reality of the Universe, so shape it well and use it wisely!

It is my hope that you find many useful gems in this herbal Book of Shadows, and develop your own magical practice using the gifts granted to us all through the abundant generosity of our beloved Earth. Blessed Be.

BASIL

As many Witches are well aware, basil is as versatile in magic as it is in the kitchen. This aromatic herb has long been used for medicinal and culinary purposes in places around the world. A beautiful annual, with its waxy green leaves and purple or white flowers, basil makes a wonderful addition to your garden or window sill and a powerful herbal ally for your magic spells.

In India, where it is known as tulsi (or "holy basil"), basil has been cultivated for over 5000 years, and it is believed to have been native to Asia, growing as far east as China. Basil was also well known to the ancient Egyptians, Greeks and Romans.

The Latin name for basil is *basilicum*, which comes from the word "basilisk"—the great serpent from ancient mythology that was said to be the king of all snakes. The Romans believed that basil was the only cure for anyone unfortunate enough to be bitten or stung by the basilisk, a superstition not far from the truth, as basil does actually have properties that relieve bites and stings from insects.

In medieval Europe, people used basil for a variety of love-related purposes, such as to determine whether a new lover would be faithful, to encourage attraction, and to soothe arguments. Continuing this tradition, basil remains one of the most commonly used herbs for love spells today. Witches also use it for luck, wealth, happiness, harmony, courage, fertility, protection, and exorcism. Basil is associated with the Element of Fire, and the planet Mars.

Today, many people enjoy basil in Italian and Southeast Asian cuisine, and the herb is easily found in both fresh and dried form in just about any grocery store. Basil is a hardy herb, so even those with rather less-than-green thumbs may want to grow their own and have the many benefits of basil available straight from the garden (or window sill).

In this chapter, you will learn how to use basil for wealth, protection, love, and courage.

SPELL FOR ATTRACTING MONEY INTO YOUR LIFE

Sometimes, no matter how well we plan, emergencies happen and ends don't quite meet. Unexpected medical costs, family emergencies, a change in employment....life can definitely throw the occasional wrench in our finances!

This simple spell helps boost your money-attracting powers to smooth out any financial wrinkles caused by unexpected events, but it's useful for any time you feel you need a little bit of extra cash. The basil leaf, with its money-attracting energies, lends its power to your personal energy.

The work begins with a quick clearing of the mind, allowing any negative thoughts that may be lurking there to be released so that they don't block your intentions from manifesting. Of course, this is a good step to take before working any magic, but it's specifically called for here in case you're actively worrying about the situation at hand, which would definitely interfere with the energy of the spell.

You will need:

- 1 fresh basil leaf
- 1 green candle
- Purse or wallet

Instructions:

Begin by taking three deep breaths. Inhale slowly through your nose, and exhale fully, releasing any negative thoughts or emotions.

Light the candle and place your purse or wallet in front of you on your altar or work space.

Hold the basil leaf between your palms and visualize a green light surrounding your purse or wallet. Let the green light wash over you as well.

Imagine your purse or wallet full of money. See yourself opening your purse or wallet to find it full of coins and bills. When you have this image firmly in your mind, say the following (or similar) words:

"Sweet basil, with energy divine,
bring the money I need to me, right on time."

Now, open your purse or wallet and gently place the basil leaf inside.

Gently extinguish the candle by waving your hand over it or using a candle snuffer. You can reuse the candle for general atmospheric lighting, or to repeat this specific spell at a later date.

Let the leaf remain in your purse or wallet for up to one week.

Be careful not to stress about how the money will show up in your life, as this interferes with the manifestation. Let the Universe sort out the "how" for you!

CLEARING THE MIND OF INADEQUACY ISSUES

We live in a fast-paced, competitive world, which can take a toll on self-esteem and self-confidence. At one time or another, anyone can feel like they don't really know what they're doing—even those who seem so well put together on the outside!

If you're dealing with a bout of the "inadequacy blues," this spell will help you clear the negative energy from your mind and get on with pursuing your dreams. With a little help from the astral realm, we can return to a balanced, confident, capable state of mind and the awareness that we can handle any obstacle life brings our way!

Herbal lore tells us that basil is a potent tool for clearing the mind when it is blocked by feelings of helplessness. Basil can help you regain your confidence, and give you the courage, strength and stamina to rise up and meet any challenge head on. In fact, as a first name, "Basil" means "brave and valiant." Use this spell to help you get in touch with your own courageous energy.

<u>You will need:</u>

- Basil essential oil
- 1 teaspoon olive oil
- Small dish
- 1 black candle
- Hand-held mirror

<u>Instructions:</u>

Before the ritual, mix a teaspoon of olive oil with a few drops of the basil essential oil in a small dish.

Begin by lighting the black candle.

Take three deep breaths. Inhale slowly through your nose, and exhale fully, releasing any negative thoughts or emotions.

Allow the energy of the black candle to rid you of any negativity in your mind or in your energy field.

Hold the mirror in your hand and gaze into your own eyes.

Gently anoint the mirror frame with the basil oil, beginning at the top and working your way around clockwise. Each time you place a small dab of oil around the frame of the mirror, repeat the following chant:

"I know who I am and I am enough."

Continue the chant as many times as you need until a warm, fresh energy flows over you.

Gently extinguish the candle and allow this new energy to infuse you as you carry on with your life.

You can always repeat the spell if you find yourself needing another boost of self-confidence.

BRINGING RECONCILIATION TO AN ESTABLISHED RELATIONSHIP

While new romantic relationships often bring a whirlwind of excitement and passion that keeps both partners feeling harmoniously toward each other, more mature relationships can easily fall into energetic ruts that lead to discord.

Once the "shine" wears off and people aren't as motivated to be on their best behavior, carelessness and neglect can creep into the day-to-day lives of even the truest of loves. Of course, all relationships require a bit of maintenance from time to time, but for a real love that lasts, a bit of magical intervention is well worth it.

Basil's energetic properties can be harnessed to bring about the peace and happiness we seek when an established relationship loses its harmonious glow. Even the scent of fresh basil is said to cause sympathy to form between two people. This spell will help you to reconnect and reconcile with your love.

<u>You will need:</u>

- 1 white candle
- 1 envelope
- Red pen
- Several small slips of paper
- 3 fresh basil leaves

<u>Instructions:</u>

Light the white candle, and take a moment to meditate on the positive qualities of your relationship.

Think about times that have been harmonious and full of ease. What details or specific feelings do you recall about those peaceful moments? What did you love the most about these times? What qualities did these times bring out in your partner that you most admire?

Using the red pen and slips of paper, write down as many details, impressions or qualities of those memories as you can.

Place them one at a time in the envelope.

When you're finished, place three basil leaves inside the envelope, and lick and seal it.

Hold the envelope in between your hands and say the following (or similar) words:

"My love for you is the sum of all of this goodness and more. Harmony between us is restored."

Place the envelope near the candle and allow the candle to burn out on its own.

Then keep the envelope in a visible place where it will remind you of the positive characteristics and qualities of your lover.

If possible, this spell can be modified to include your partner so that you can do it together. This is especially ideal for couples who live together.

Each of you should write several qualities that you find important and special in the other person and place the slips of paper into the envelope.

Repeat the words of the spell together, then place the envelope where you both can see it.

SPELL FOR WELCOMING THE START OF A RELATIONSHIP

If you're an intuitive person, you've almost certainly been in this situation at least once: you meet someone new, notice a spark between the two of you, and can just tell that something is about to happen.

For most of us, this sets in motion a period of heightened awareness, a bit (or a lot!) of fantasizing about the other person, butterflies in the stomach, and many other signs and symptoms of an oncoming romantic relationship.

This period of time can be fun, but also truly challenging, especially when you just really want to know how it's all going to turn out. It can be very tempting to try to help things along with a little magic.

The less enlightened magical practitioners among us might simply cast a spell to make *sure* that the initial spark turns into an exciting romance. However, the all-important principle of "*harm none*" comes into play here.

It is actually harmful to interfere with someone else's free will by casting love spells that attempt to control how they feel. If you think about it, you probably wouldn't want the same done to you!

What's more, relationships that arise from successful manipulative love spells are doomed to fall apart sooner or later, since the feelings they are based on are not true and pure. Who wants to deal with the drama of a magically manipulated relationship when authentic, healthy and honest relationships are so much better?

This spell provides an alternative method for making the most of the spark you've recently discovered, without getting into less-than-ethical territory. The intention is to declare to the Universe that 1) you are receptive and ready for a romantic relationship, and 2) you desire that the connection with this new person manifests according to the highest good for all involved.

Of course, this means that you're open to the possibility that this spark will *not* evolve into a relationship. But since welcoming the start of a relationship is the focus of this spell, you are still setting an intention to find new romance. You never know—it could be that this new person actually ends up introducing you to your next love, who ignites an even bigger spark! The point is to focus on *what* you want, rather than *who* you want, and let the Universe take care of the details.

<u>You will need:</u>

- 3 sprigs of basil
- 1 pink ribbon
- Small vase
- Cup of water

Instructions:

Visualize yourself confident and at ease around the person with whom you are hoping to start a relationship. Imagine the two of you in as much detail as possible, sitting side by side in a sunny location.

Breathe deeply and summon a feeling of peace and ease around this person.

Pour water from the cup into the vase.

Now take one sprig of basil and place it into the vase and say, "*My authentic self shines through in this new connection.*"

Place the second sprig of basil in the vase and say, "*My authentic self resonates with the authentic self of the one I love.*"

Place the final sprig of basil in the vase and say, "*This new connection serves the highest good of all involved.*"

Now, wrap the pink ribbon around the three sprigs of basil.

Spend a few moments imagining how you want to feel in your next relationship, but keep the focus on yourself, rather than on the person you're hoping to be with.

Hold the vase in your hands and say, "*I welcome the start of this new relationship, for the good of all and harm to none.*"

Make sure the vase has plenty of fresh water each day.

When the sprigs begin to droop or turn brown, take them outside and scatter them over the Earth.

BAY LAUREL (BAY LEAF)

Used widely as a flavor boost for soups and sauces, the leaf of the bay laurel tree is also a useful ally in magic. In fact, this herb is often referred to simply as "bay leaf," since this is the main part of the plant utilized in both cooking and spellwork, though the bark is sometimes used in medicinal healing.

Historical records show us that bay was sacred to Apollo, the Greek god of healing. Ancient myths tell of how Apollo fell desperately in love with the nymph Daphne, daughter of Earth goddess Gaia and river god Peneus. When Daphne did not return Apollo's feelings, because she had vowed to remain unmarried, Apollo appeared to be ready to pursue her forever.

She asked her father for help, and he turned her into a bay tree to keep her safe. Apollo declared that if he could not marry Daphne, he would honor her tree forever, and he gently harvested some of the bay tree's leaves to decorate his magical harp and to wear as a crown. Thereafter, the bay leaf was a symbol of devotion and of victory, as seen in many paintings depicting ancient Greek society, where highly respected people often wore crowns of laurel.

Bay laurel was also worn for protection against vengeance from angry gods, and for the healing properties attributed to it by some ancient physicians. This dual reputation for protective and curative powers lasted well into the Middle Ages, when bay leaves were used in spells to protect people from the plague, as well as from negative magic of all kinds.

Bay laurel is associated with the Element of Fire and the Sun. Its magical purposes include money, good fortune and success, as well as healing and purification. The wide, flat shape of the leaf makes it excellent for writing wishes on in spellwork. Bay is also used in many protection spells, as well as for divination and clairvoyance.

Below, you'll find spells to bring about prophetic dreams, athletic success, protection from psychic attack, and banishing negativity from the home.

PROPHETIC DREAM SACHET

Dreams are considered the gateway to the subconscious. In our sleep, we are often more open to messages from the Universe than we are in waking life. Yet it can be difficult to remember our dreams, or to make much sense of them even when we do remember, as they can often seem trivial or nonsensical. This is especially true when we're living very busy lives with a lot on our minds.

But even if this is the case, you can improve the clarity of your dreams and your ability to recall them with a regular habit of recording your dreams first thing in the morning. And you can even set an intention to receive knowledge of future events through your dreams, which this spell will help you do.

This spell draws on bay leaf's association with divination and clairvoyance, encouraging an open channel between your dreaming brain and any messages that may be waiting for you in the etheric realm. However, the writing component is as important as the spellwork itself, as it's only through recording and reflecting on these dreams that you can start to see patterns, make observations, and take any necessary actions that will bring about positive change in your life.

Train yourself to begin writing as soon as possible after waking, recording everything you remember, as connections can emerge from seemingly random details. Over time, the habit of recording your dreams will also help you remember more and more.

This spell is best done regularly over the course of several weeks, or until you've established a regular habit of remembering and recording your dreams. If you find that you've gone more than a few days without any significant dreams, try repeating the spell.

You will need:

- 3 bay leaves
- 1 small drawstring bag
- Silver ribbon
- Journal or notebook
- Pen (or pencil)

Instructions:

Begin by sitting in bed.

Place the bay leaves, small sachet, and silver ribbon on a tray or nightstand.

You may want to do some meditating, drink some calming tea, or any other activity that helps your brain prepare for sleep.

When you're ready, hold the bay leaves between your palms and speak aloud your intentions for the night's dreams.

If there is a specific situation you want assistance with, such as an issue with work or a loved one, clearly define your question. You can also just ask for general guidance.

Once you've made your request, place the bay leaves inside the drawstring bag and tie it with the silver ribbon.

Place the bay leaf sachet under your pillow and go to sleep.

Keep the journal and pen near your bed so that you can record your dream first thing after waking.

ATHLETIC SUCCESS SPELL

Whether you're running a marathon, competing in an intramural sports league, or simply wanting to establish a new workout routine, this spell can kickstart the energy you need to achieve your goal.

Traditionally, bay laurel is the herb of athletic power, and the fulfillment of wishes for glory in victory. The color red is associated with vitality, strength, competition and courage, making the candle an important component to the work.

Try this spell on the eve of any important event involving physical activity.

<u>You will need:</u>

- 1 bay leaf
- Red candle
- Small heat-proof glass dish
- Permanent marker

<u>Instructions:</u>

Light the candle and spend a few moments visualizing a successful outcome to your endeavor. This may mean being the first to cross the finish line, holding a winner's trophy, or just walking out of the gym feeling energized and refreshed.

Now, choose an action word—a verb—that represents the essence of the activity you're partaking in. It could be "run," "focus," "breathe," "win," or any other word that holds power for you and makes you feel motivated.

When you have your word, use the marker to write it on the bay leaf.

Hold the leaf over the candle flame and say the following (or similar) words:

"For the good of all, with harm to none
my victory is already won."

Now carefully ignite the leaf and place it in the small glass dish to burn.

Inhale the aroma and visualize yourself calm, focused and energized as you undertake your athletic activity.

Leave the candle to burn out on its own.

Sprinkle the ashes of the bay leaf onto the Earth.

PROTECTION FROM PSYCHIC ATTACK

The phrase "psychic attack" can refer to many different things, up to and including harmful magic aimed at a specific person. While the belief that one has been "cursed" by another is generally regarded as old-fashioned superstition, the resurgence of interest in magic in the 21st century means that this is, unfortunately, a real possibility.

Yet most of the time psychic attacks are unintentional, caused by hostile or otherwise negative feelings on the part of people we're having some sort of conflict with. A psychic attack can also result from simply being in the vicinity of impersonal, unattached negative thought forms, such as those found in places where tragedies have occurred.

Witches tend to be extra sensitive by nature, and are therefore able to detect negative energies that may be hanging around, whether or not we have any clue as to the source. If you've been feeling negatively affected by some kind of outside influence, try wearing or carrying this charm, which combines the protective energies of bay leaf and the number six.

If you can, take a purifying ritual bath to remove any unwanted energies around yourself before working this spell.

You will need:

- 6 bay leaves
- 1 black candle
- Small drawstring bag

Instructions:

Light the black candle and visualize all negativity being sucked up by the flame of the candle and disappearing.

When you sense that your magical space is free of negativity, take a bay leaf in your hand and hold it up.

While drawing a circle around yourself with the leaf, say the following (or similar) words:

"From the divine powers of the Earth and Sun, this leaf is my shield and my protection."

Place the bay leaf inside the drawstring bag. Repeat this with each of the remaining leaves.

When all six leaves are in the bag, hold it above your head and visualize the leaves casting a white sphere around you as protection from any harmful energy.

Each day, pin the charm to the inside of your clothing or carry it in your pocket until you feel that protection is no longer needed.

BANISHING NEGATIVITY FROM THE HOME: A GROUP SPELL

This spell is for roommates or family members who have been experiencing frequent arguments, moodiness, or any other kind of disharmony around the home.

Of course, if there are active interpersonal conflicts causing the negativity, these will need to be resolved through honest and respectful dialogue. You may find that this is more easily achieved after working this spell together, or you may need to discuss the issue(s) first and then work the spell.

No matter what the situation, it's important that every member of the group is fully willing to participate in the work. If someone is going along with it reluctantly, their energy is likely to weaken the effects of the spell.

<u>You will need:</u>

- 1 dried bay leaf per person
- 1 small slip of paper per person
- 1 6-inch length of pink thread per person
- Small drawstring bag
- Pink marker
- Work candle (optional)

<u>Instructions:</u>

Begin by having all the members of the household come together in a small circle. Light the candle, if using.

Collectively count three deep breaths to relax and focus the energy of the group.

Passing the marker from person to person, each will use it to write their name on their slip of paper.

After all the names are written down, each person will gently roll their slip of paper with their bay leaf and tie it with a length of pink thread.

This is done one person at a time, while the rest of the group visualizes the person feeling safe and at peace within the house.

Once everyone has rolled and tied their paper and leaf, have each person place theirs inside the drawstring bag.

Pull the bag closed after all the leaves are in.

Once again, pass the bag around to each person in the circle. Have each person hold it between their palms and say, "*I am held in light and love within this house.*"

While doing this, each person should visualize a pink glow around the circle, concentrating on safety and love.

When everyone has held the bag and spoken, hang it near an entrance to your home where all will be reminded of this special group working.

CHAMOMILE

The tiny, daisy-like flowers of the chamomile plant have long been recognized for their magical, medicinal and cosmetic properties. Of course, Witches frequently use chamomile in the same way most other people do—to unwind with a cup of chamomile tea—but there are plenty of other uses for this delightful herb as well.

Chamomile was first cultivated in ancient Egypt, where it was used as a cosmetic, a cure for fever, and a key ingredient in embalming fluids used for the pharaohs. The ancient Greeks called this herb "chamaimēlon," meaning "Earth apple," for its low-growing height and mildly sweet fragrance.

The Saxons called it "maythen," and included it among their nine sacred herbs. The ancient Norse added chamomile to shampoo to brighten their hair. In Medieval times, chamomile petals were strewn around at social gatherings to create a pleasant odor, and chamomile was even used to flavor beer before hops were adopted for that purpose.

As an herb associated both with the Sun and the Element of Water, chamomile has unique dual powers. For example, you can both balance your vital energy and calm your mental stress with chamomile tea or essential oil. Similarly, in any spell that requires a psychic clearing of the space to remove unwanted energies, chamomile serves a double function—to drive away negativity and replace it with the powerful brightness and sustaining strength of the Sun.

While chamomile is primarily known for its ability to promote healing and peaceful sleep and reduce stress, it has several other magical uses, including love, purification, prosperity, and good luck in gambling. This herb is also known as an all-around spell booster, making it a good candidate for substitutions if you're wanting to work a particular spell but don't have the exact ingredients.

In this chapter, you'll learn to use chamomile to magically decrease your stress, boost your luck, release old emotional baggage, and get much-needed rest during challenging times.

ENERGY RESET SPELL

Chamomile's dual energies of Fire (planetary association) and Water (Elemental association) make it an excellent tool for neutralizing unpleasant energy and increasing positive feelings simultaneously.

In this meditative spell, the calming attributes of chamomile tea are harnessed, but with a twist—the herb is applied to closed eyes rather than imbibed. Of course, you can always enjoy a nice hot cup of chamomile to help you balance your energies, but try this spell at least once as well—you'll be amazed at how well it "resets" your mind!

You will need:

- 2 chamomile tea bags
- Washcloth or small towel
- Medium-sized bowl
- Warm water
- Journal or writing paper (optional)
- Work candle for atmosphere (optional)

Instructions:

Light the candle, if using.

Place the tea bags and washcloth in the bowl.

Heat some water (no need to bring it all the way to a boil) in order to warm the tea bags.

While you wait for the water to warm, make a mental list of positive feelings you want to bring into your life at this time. For example, you may be struggling to find patience or forgiveness regarding a specific situation, or you may just want to feel peaceful and serene.

Next, make a mental list of the things that you would like to release from your life, such as frustration, stress, anxiety, negative thoughts, etc. You may want to write these lists on a small slip of paper to help you recall them in the next step of the spell.

Once the water has begun to steam, pour it over the tea bags and washcloth and let them soak until they are warmed throughout, but not too hot to touch.

Find a comfortable place to lie down or sit in a reclined position with your eyes closed.

Place one tea bag over each eye and gently drape the washcloth across both eyes so that it also touches your forehead and the bridge of your nose.

Take a few deep breaths, and then begin the transmutation of negativity into positivity by releasing what you want to be rid of on the exhale, and attracting what you want to feel on the inhale, using the lists you made earlier to guide you.

Each time you breathe in say (aloud or silently to yourself), "*I bring [patience] into my life.*"

Each time you exhale, think or say "*I release [needless worry] from my life.*"

You can try moving completely through each of your lists, or you might feel drawn to focusing on one particular set of words. Follow your intuition here—what do you really need to release, and what do you truly want to attract?

Once the tea bags and washcloth have cooled, remove them from your face.

Take a deep breath, inhaling all the positive feelings and experiences you have focused on and bring your renewed sense of peace with you for the rest of the day.

LUCKY SEVENS: A SPELL FOR GAMES OF CHANCE

It is well known that many gamblers and gamers employ lucky charms to increase their mojo. Traditionally, washing one's hands in chamomile-infused water is believed to lend good luck to the gambler.

Whether you're planning a trip to the casino, or just heading out for a friendly game of poker with friends, give this spell a try. Just be sure not to use the dice in any actual game, as you don't want your lucky charm to absorb other peoples' energies.

Instead, keep them in your pocket as you play. And be sure to share at least a small portion of your winnings with someone else, as this will increase your luck for the next occasion!

You will need:

- 1 chamomile tea bag
- Hot water
- Medium-sized bowl
- Hand towel
- Pair of dice

Instructions:

Before the ritual, place a pair of dice face up on your altar that add up to seven (1 and 6, 2 and 5, or 3 and 4).

Brew a cup of pure chamomile tea and let it cool to the touch.

Carefully pour the chamomile tea into a medium sized bowl while visualizing a white or silver light flowing around your body.

When the water in the bowl is cool enough, place your hands in it and rub them together vigorously.

Visualize yourself in the situation in which you want to be lucky. See yourself having a good time, and smiling as you carry off your winnings.

If you want to increase the abundant energy of the spell, imagine how you will share some of those winnings with others—whether by buying a round of drinks, leaving a very generous tip at a restaurant, or donating a little to charity.

When you have finished with your visualization, dry your hands on the hand towel and immediately pick up the dice.

Hold them between your palms and say the following (or similar) words:

"Lucky sevens, lucky dice,
winning always feels so nice.
Lucky sevens, lucky pair,
as I win, I also share.
So mote it be."

Place the dice in your pocket or purse and bring them to your gambling event.

RELEASING NEGATIVE ENERGY FROM AN ENDED RELATIONSHIP

The end of a relationship is rarely simple. Even if it ends mutually and on good terms, negative or otherwise unresolved energy from past relationships can linger for months or even years.

After a relationship ends, many people experience feelings of insecurity, anger, sadness or simply disappointment. This is a normal part of the grieving process, but some people find themselves unable to move on even after a reasonable amount of time has passed.

This spell uses the calming, clarifying power of chamomile to help you release any lingering relationship negativity so you can regain your full sovereignty, independence and strength. You may want to do some journaling in preparation for this work, especially if you sense that there are unexamined issues surrounding your feelings about the relationship.

You will need:

- 1 light blue or violet candle
- 1 cup hot chamomile tea
- Small strip of paper
- Journal or writing paper (optional)
- Fire-proof dish

Instructions:

Light the candle and prepare the tea.

If necessary, do some journaling about the feelings and thoughts you wish to release.

You can begin drinking the tea as you write.

When you feel you've arrived at a point of clarity, write your name and the other person's name on the strip of paper.

Hold the mug of tea in both hands and breathe in while saying to yourself, *"My mind is clear."*

On the exhale, visualize the all unwanted energy leaving your spirit and mind. You may want to visualize your thoughts and feelings about the relationship as a dark grey cloud and blow the cloud away.

Now set the mug down and take the strip of paper in your dominant hand.

Ignite it with the candle flame and drop it into the fire-proof dish to burn out.

As you do so, say out loud, "*I am letting my relationship with [name of person] go now.*"

Continue to sip your tea until it's finished, and then gently extinguish the candle.

Scatter the ashes from the strip of paper onto the Earth or into a running stream.

PEACEFUL SLEEP SACHET FOR DIFFICULT TIMES

At times of peak stress, quality sleep is more vital than ever. But of course, these are often the times when sleep is hard to come by. Chamomile's restorative, peace-bringing properties, along with its ability to dispel negative energy makes it an excellent herb to rely on when the going gets rough.

If you can't find a drawstring bag in light blue, you can sew your own sachet from any light blue cloth. Try to use light, breathe-able fabric in order to make the most of chamomile's scent. The essential oil is optional, but if you have or can purchase it, it will boost the effectiveness of this spell enormously.

It's ideal to work this one as close to bedtime as possible—even while sitting in bed, if you can. But by all means, don't let timing considerations stop you from creating this very useful spell craft!

<u>You will need:</u>

- 3 tablespoons dried chamomile flowers
- Small light-blue drawstring bag or square of cloth
- Chamomile essential oil (optional)

<u>Instructions:</u>

Prepare for sleep as you normally would, then spend a few moments taking long, deep breaths, focusing on the inhalation and exhalation until your mind has quieted some.

Fill the drawstring bag with the dried chamomile flowers and buds.

If using, tap three drops of chamomile essential oil into the sachet.

Inhale gently and allow the earthy, sweet scent of the chamomile to further relax you.

Press the sachet between your hands and gently roll it to release more of the chamomile scent.

Say the following (or similar) words three times:

"Peaceful sleep, stress be gone, gentle rest until the dawn."

Place the sachet next to your pillow and lie down.

Relax your legs, arms, shoulders, hands, neck, and jaw.

Visualize yourself being suspended by a light blue mist, which supports and envelops you as you sink into a deep relaxed state and then drift into a peaceful sleep.

CINNAMON

Cinnamon is another herb commonly found in our kitchens that actually has a long history of both culinary and magical importance. Anyone familiar with its pungent taste and scent will probably not be surprised to learn that cinnamon is associated with the Sun and the Element of Fire, but it's actually also an Air herb, lending it more versatility than you might suspect.

Like chamomile, cinnamon was used in the embalming process of the ancient Egyptians. It was also burned as an incense in the temples of the gods, a custom that continued in the temples of ancient Greece and Rome. For hundreds of years, Arabic peoples transported cinnamon from its native Asia to Europe, all the while keeping its origins a secret, in order to maintain high prices for the coveted spice.

Traders crafted tall tales about the dangers of obtaining the exotic sticks of cinnamon, which were said to be guarded by huge falcon-like birds or terrifying giant snakes. The rarity and price of cinnamon made it a status symbol among Europeans all the way up to the 16th century, and the discovery of new routes for acquiring cinnamon and other exotic spices was a chief goal of explorers like Columbus.

Fortunately for us, cinnamon is now widely available, not just as a spice but as an incense and an energetic ally in meeting various magical goals. Its aphrodisiac qualities make it excellent for spells involving love and the libido, and ancient texts from Europe, Egypt, and China note its power to draw in happiness.

Cinnamon is also an excellent ingredient in spells to increase your financial and personal prosperity, as these successes are also linked to the bright-hot power of the Sun. Many Witches add a piece of cinnamon stick to magical sachets aimed at manifesting success, money, protection and more, as its fiery properties can add an extra "kick" to just about any working.

Finally, the powerful heat of cinnamon is strong in its ability to shine positive light into dark corners—whether of a physical dwelling or of the mind. As such, this herb is perfect for banishing stagnant negativity and providing protection.

In this chapter, you will find spells using cinnamon to consecrate your ritual tools, improve the energy of your living space, and bring about healing.

WINTER HEARTH AND HOME CHARMS

In Northern climates, we spend more time indoors during winter than any other time of year. This makes it especially important to have positive energy in the home.

These festive decorations are reminiscent of Yule and the warm, cheerful essence of the holiday season. Pine cones carry the cleansing, protective and healing attributes of the pine tree and add joyful energy to the home. The scent of cinnamon evokes warmth and coziness—just the things you want to experience when sheltering from the cold, dark weeks of winter.

Hand-gathered pine cones from the outdoors are ideal, but if need be you can purchase them from a craft store.

<u>You will need:</u>

- Large bowl
- 3-5 pinecones
- White glue
- Paint brush
- Powdered cinnamon

Instructions:

Before you begin, take a moment to appreciate the earthy and pungent scents of the pine cones and cinnamon.

Say some words of gratitude to the Earth for her bounty. You might say, *"Thank you, Mother Earth, for providing me with these beautiful pinecones from your evergreen trees."*

Use the paint brush to cover one pine cone with the glue while focusing on your intention for a peaceful, happy environment in your home.

Once the cone is sufficiently coated with glue, sprinkle on the cinnamon.

Place in an upright position to allow the pine cone to fully dry.

Repeat with each successive pine cone, continuing to visualize joyful, peaceful feelings.

When all the pine cones are cinnamon-coated and dried, place them in a large bowl.

Take a moment to hold the bowl in your hands as you picture joyful, serene energy circling your home.

Say the following (or similar) words:

"Hearth and home on winter's night
Filled with joy and peaceful light."

Place the bowl in a room in your home where the pine cones will be visible. Alternatively, you might spread them throughout the house, placing one pine cone in each room.

NEW HOME BLESSING AND PROTECTION SPELL

Most people are aware of the benefits of smudging a new home with sage, lavender, and/or other herbs before moving bringing in their belongings. But it's also important to "set the tone," energetically speaking, once you've unpacked and begun to settle in.

Think of this spell as putting the "finishing touches" on your new dwelling place, as you both protect your space and call in beneficial, joyful energies.

<u>You will need:</u>

- Cinnamon essential oil
- White vinegar
- Funnel
- Spray bottle
- Sponge or cloth
- White candle
- Portable candle holder

<u>Instructions:</u>

Mix one cup of water with ten to fifteen drops of cinnamon oil and pour it into the spray bottle with the funnel. Fill the remaining portion of the spray bottle with white vinegar.

Place the white candle in a safe, portable holder so that you are able to carry it around the house with you.

Light the candle as you visualize your entire home being suffused with white light.

Beginning with the door you use most to enter the house, spray the sponge or cloth with the cinnamon mixture and wipe down both sides of the door.

Visualize yourself creating a magical barrier between your home and any unwanted energies.

Repeat this process as you walk around, in a clockwise motion, to spray and wipe each door and window frame in your home.

When you have finished with all the doors and window, sit quietly for a moment and envision a white light connecting all windows and doors, enveloping your entire house and protecting it.

You may want to say the following (or similar) words:

"Within these walls, I am protected, blessed, and joyful.
So let it be."

Leave the candle in a safe place to burn out on its own.

BLUES-BANISHING SPELL

There are many physical remedies and preventive strategies—such as healthy diet and exercise—to address mild depression. But adding in a bit of magic can go a long way toward lifting you out of a case of the doldrums. This spell draws on cinnamon's bright, sunny aspect, in combination with the clearing powers of its Air aspect, to help you realign after a slump.

If you can, play some relaxing music or nature sounds while working this spell. It isn't strictly necessary, but sound therapy is a powerful healer and should be taken advantage of if at all possible!

<u>You will need:</u>

- 1 stick or cone of cinnamon incense
- Incense holder
- Yellow spell candle
- Relaxing music (optional)

<u>Instructions:</u>

Find a place to sit or lie down where you can relax and will not be disturbed.

Light the candle and the cinnamon incense.

Say the following (or similar words) aloud:

"I choose to release any unwanted feelings and raise my vibration to a higher frequency."

Now, close your eyes and take some time to concentrate on the earthy, pungent smell of the cinnamon.

Visualize yourself surrounded with a happy, loving white light.

Take long, slow deep breaths and see any sadness or anxiety as a thick smoke that releases from your body as you exhale.

On the inhale, bring in the strong white light and allow it to infuse your whole body.

Continue this visualization until you feel significantly lighter, or until the candle has completely burned away.

Repeat daily as needed until you're back in balance on the physical, emotional and spiritual levels.

CINNAMON ANOINTING / CONSECRATION OIL

While it's a fun and time-honored art to create your own magical oil blends, the DIY route isn't always practical, especially for Witches just starting out in the Craft. This simple, "single serve" recipe is a nice alternative for those without the time or supplies needed to create and store a more complex, longer-lasting batch. Cinnamon's vibrant energy and powerful scent makes it a great choice for a single anointing oil, whether you're using it in a candle spell or to consecrate your ritual tools.

Since you won't be storing the leftover oil (unless you have a very small bottle!), you may want to make the most of it by consecrating several objects at once. You might make a practice of gathering all your magical tools around you at the beginning of each season of the year to re-focus your energies, re-consecrate your tools, and bless and consecrate any new additions.

<u>You will need:</u>

- 1 teaspoon olive oil

- 3 drops cinnamon essential oil
- Small dish
- Ritual tools / magical items

Instructions:

After gathering the items you wish to consecrate, place the small dish at the center of your table or altar.

Mix three drops of cinnamon essential oil and the olive oil in the dish and gently stir to combine.

As you do this, visualize yourself as a conduit of energy between the Universe/the Goddess and God/the spiritual realm (however you understand "higher power") and the oil itself.

Take a few moments to breathe deeply and quiet your mind.

When feel ready, begin consecrating your tools.

Hold each object one at a time in your hand.

Dip your finger in the oil and touch it to your object while you say the following (or similar) words:

"In the light of the Sun and Moon,
in the name of the Elements of Earth, Air, Water and Fire,
in the presence of Spirit,
of the Goddess and the God,
I dedicate you to divine purpose.
Blessed Be."

Repeat this process with each object.

When you're finished, take a moment to align your energy with your objects.

Imagine your energy as a gentle, glowing light, radiating from you to surround each object until it also pulses softly with your energy.

When you feel this has been accomplished, return your tools and other magical items to their proper places.

DANDELION

Dandelion, from the French "dent de lion," or "tooth of the lion" is in our modern times considered a "weed," and many homeowners despair every year as the bright yellow heads threaten to take over the lawn. But this ubiquitous herb actually has amazing magical, medicinal, and yes, even culinary powers.

Up until a decade or so ago, dandelion was never associated with food, but finally the discovery of the dandelion leaf as a delicious addition to salads has become fairly widely known. This same leaf, along with the root of the plant, is also an excellent diuretic and cleanser. Teas and tonics with dandelion will cleanse the kidneys and liver in particular, and detox soups made with dandelion will help with bloating and other digestive difficulties. The sap from the stems can even be used to cure warts!

Magically, dandelion is known as an herb of "wish fulfillment," perhaps at least in part due to the age-old tradition of making a wish and then blowing on the seed head (or "puff") of an old white dandelion. It is also strongly associated with psychic powers, divination and the spirit world. Dandelion tea is imbibed to increase psychic ability, aid in divination and in bringing on prophetic dreams.

Perhaps in recognition of their ease of propagation, and the fact that it is one of the earliest signs that Spring has arrived, many Pagan traditions associate dandelion with growth and transformation, with adaptability, and "blooming where you are planted." Dandelion is associated with Jupiter and the element of Air.

Dandelion is a great illustration of the benefits of listening to your own true voice, and allowing yourself to become confident in your magical abilities. Magic at its best will cause you to see the world with magical eyes. So the next time you see a dandelion patch in your yard or in a field, let go of the notion of "pesky weeds" and embrace this mighty yet humble gift of Nature for what it is—an ally in pursuit of health, wisdom, and happiness.

In the following pages, you'll find spells to help you find balance, increase psychic clarity, release unwanted habits, and make a wish come true.

WISH-GRANTING SPELL

Dandelion has long been known as the wish-fulfillment herb. This simple, elegant spell is meant to be tailored to most magical goals, though it helps to be realistic if you want to see success.

In other words, wishing for a million dollars to show up on your doorstep tomorrow is unlikely to produce results. Wishing for extra money to come from an unexpected source, on the other hand, is likely to succeed, provided you have sufficient focus on your intention. For those just starting out with magic, this is a great spell to "start small" with, in order to build your confidence.

Choose an herb and a color with magical associations related to your goal. There are plenty of resources out there to help you with this, including this guide, if you need correspondence information.

<u>You will need:</u>

- 1 spell candle, color corresponding to your wish
- ½ teaspoon dandelion root
- ½ teaspoon herb corresponding to your wish

<u>Instructions:</u>

Spend a few quiet moments visualizing your wish having already manifested. How will you feel when this magical goal is met? Focus on calling up feelings of joy, excitement, gratitude—whatever feels appropriate, depending on the nature of the wish.

Arrange the wish-associated herb in a circle, moving clockwise around the candle holder, continuing to visualize your goal. Then arrange the dandelion root in an outer circle (also clockwise).

Now, light the candle as you say the following (or similar) words:

"[Name of herb] and dandelion, so enchanted
As the candle burns, my wish is granted."

Leave the candle to burn out on its own. Sprinkle the herbs outdoors, over the Earth.

PSYCHIC CLARITY SPELL

At some point or other, we all experience dilemmas that we can't find an immediate solution for. The mind often goes into analytical overdrive at times like this, as we draw on our instincts for problem solving, to no avail. Eventually, the mind can create so much "noise" over the issue that it's impossible to think clearly, let alone be open to intuitive ideas that might be available to us from the spiritual plane.

Dandelion has long been known to assist in opening and clarifying the third eye—the seat of intuition. This spell will help you quiet the "monkey mind" and open up to psychic messages.

Although prepackaged dandelion tea has become increasingly available, it's ideal to use loose, dried and cut dandelion leaves (available at many natural food stores) for this particular spell. You can place them in a tea strainer, or—even better—brew them loose and leave them to sink to the bottom of the mug.

<u>You will need:</u>

- Purple, lavender, blue or silver candle
- 1-2 teaspoons dried dandelion leaves
- Tea strainer (optional)
- Mug
- Journal or writing paper

Instructions:

First, let go of your need to have an answer to your problem right this minute. This may seem counter-intuitive, but if you are to be open to messages from the invisible realms, you need to be calm and in a receptive mode.

Light the candle and prepare the tea. Allow the leaves to steep for five to ten minutes.

Take several deep breaths to relax and focus.

Before taking your first sip of tea, say the following (or similar) words:

"I am open to all possibilities.
I trust my guides to show me the way
In perfect timing, and for the good of all."

Now you may begin to reflect on your situation, but do so with an open mind and trust that the solution will eventually become clear.

Talk to the spirit realm, whether this means the Goddess and God, the Universe, your personal guides, or however you understand a higher power. Speak aloud if possible.

You will find that thoughts will come into your consciousness. Do not reject anything out of hand—simply explore the ideas with an open mind, no matter how silly or strange you think they might be. If you like, write down anything that feels even remotely significant.

If, by the time you've finished the tea, nothing has crystallized for you yet, simply extinguish the candle and let go of the issue. Return to your written notes in a day or two, and see what is starting to make sense. You may have to wait a few days to get your answer.

In the meantime, you can continue to relight the candle over successive nights until it is spent.

SUN AND MOON BALANCE SPELL

Human beings live such busy lives; sometimes it seems we should be called "human doings," for we often forget to take the time to *be*. Too much activity, without the counteracting energies of rest, can lead to all kinds of physical, emotional and even spiritual imbalance, though.

It's important to balance these masculine, yang, Sun energies with the feminine, yin influence of the Moon. On the flip side, too much yin energy can lead to lethargy and stagnation, so it's important to have the counterbalancing energy of action.

Dandelion is considered a symbol of balance due to its dual appearances. It resembles the Sun when in flower, and the white globe of the Moon when it becomes a seed head. This spell draws on the energies of dandelion, the Sun and the Moon to help you assess your state of balance and what you might do to improve it if need be.

<u>You will need:</u>

- Silver candle
- Gold candle
- Dandelion flower petals
- Piece of paper
- Pen
- Envelope

<u>Instructions:</u>

Place the piece of paper on your altar or table.

Draw a line down the middle of the page.

Label one side "Sun (Activities)" and the other "Moon (Relaxation)."

Place the gold candle on the Sun side and light it. Take a moment to reflect on all the things that you do in terms of work, social life, family, and any other commitments you have. Write them on the Sun side of your list.

Place the silver candle on the Moon side and light it. Take a moment to reflect on all the ways you relax and care for yourself, both in solitude and with others. Write them on the Moon side of your list.

Take a moment to meditate on the balance of this list. Where might you need to increase or decrease your activity or relaxation in order to bring harmony into your life? How might you make some adjustments in order to achieve better balance?

When you are done, fold the paper and place it in the envelope.

Sprinkle dandelion petals inside, giving silent thanks to the flower for its balancing energies.

Seal the envelope with a drop of silver and gold wax from the candles. In two months or so, return to your list and see what changes have been made in your life.

SPELL FOR LETTING GO OF AN UNWANTED HABIT

Many Wiccans, Witches, and other magic practitioners say that as their practices have developed, they've felt less and less comfortable with "bad" habits that they've had for a long time. When you find yourself ready to face the challenge of expelling an unwanted habit from your life, dandelion's properties of transformation and adaptability can help.

This spell helps you to focus your mind, crystallize your thoughts and feelings around the habit, and visualize the benefits of living free from its grip. The color black is traditionally associated with banishing unwanted influences.

The fact that dandelion appears in early spring makes it a symbol of cleansing and renewal. Obviously, you will only be able to work this spell in spring and summer months, and you'll need to find dandelions in their "puff ball," or seed head stage. But these factors, requiring an extra degree of planning, only contribute to your committed intention for the goal.

This spell is ideally performed outdoors on a calm day, but you can also work near an open door or window if need be.

You will need:

- Black candle
- Candle holder safe for outdoor use
- 1 or more dandelions in seed head stage

Instructions:

Take a few moments to breathe deeply and calm your mind. Ideally (if you're outdoors), place your hands on the grass or dirt, and feel the steady presence of the Earth as you breathe.

Light the black candle and hold a dandelion in your hand. Take a moment to reflect on the habit you wish to release.

Consider how feeling bound by the habit affects you. As you call up these negative feelings—guilt, shame, helplessness, etc.—surrounding the habit, imagine placing them on the head of the dandelion as you hold it.

Allow your magical self to infuse the dandelion with all that you want to be rid of in relation to this habit. Take a deep breath and say the following (or similar) words:

"I transform into who I wish to be.
I adapt to necessary changes.
I am free from unwanted behavior.
Blessed Be."

Take another deep breath and blow away the white dandelion puff, imagining the unwanted habit breaking up into all of its negative associations and effects, scattering to the wind, never to bother you again.

You may wish to repeat this a few times, depending on the severity of the habit and the number of dandelions you were able to gather.

When you have finished, collect the stems of the dandelions and bury them back into the Earth.

You can repeat this spell as many times as you need.

ELECAMPANE

Also known as scabwort, elf dock, wild sunflower and velvet dock, elecampane was known with great affection by ancient Roman poets as "inula," a name believed to be related to the Greek name "Helenium." Indeed, legend associates it with Helen, wife of Menelaus, who had her hands full of this herb when Paris stole her away.

Another legend states that it sprang from the tears Helen wept during this abduction. Pliny the elder noted that, when chewed, inula fortified the teeth. An Ancient Latin saying proclaims: *Enula campana reddit praecordia sana* ("Elecampane will the spirits sustain"). And apparently medieval monks agreed with this sentiment, as they favored elecampane as a cordial!

In Victorian London, elecampane was sold in a candied cake, recommended for soothing asthmatic complaints. In modern herbal medicine, elecampane can be a powerful stimulant for those suffering from respiratory problems, as it reaches deeply into the lungs, allowing the body to thin out infections and fight them more effectively.

Similarly, on a spiritual level, elecampane is a powerful herb for openings, as it penetrates through old, rooted griefs so they may be processed and released. The root in particular is very useful for initiating the first stages of healing.

Witches have traditionally used elecampane in spells for protection against disease, to promote good luck, and to attract healthy love relationships. It is also an excellent assistant for enhancing communication with the spirit world. Linked with the planet Mercury and the element of Air, elecampane can stir things up and offer a new beginning after experiences of grief or despair, especially when one has been in those lower vibrational states for an extended period of time.

The spells in this chapter use elecampane to help you connect with Elemental spirits, open up to new love, ease homesickness, and clear your work environment from negative energy caused by gossip or other ill-intentioned communications.

SPELL TO EASE HOMESICKNESS

This spell is good for those who have recently moved and are missing their old friends, family, routines and patterns. Getting accustomed to a new living environment takes time, and "homesickness" can flare up often, and over a longer period of time than you might expect. This is especially true if the move wasn't desired, but had to occur due to career or family reasons.

Elecampane root's soothing energies can help to heal the emotional upheaval of being uprooted from one's home. This spell helps shift the mind from a focus on what has been lost to a focus on what can be eternally appreciated about the people and places one has left behind.

Note: this spell involves a more elaborate method for herb burning than the typical incense sticks or cones. Use extra caution with each step below. You can find self-igniting charcoal at metaphysical stores or online.

You will need:

- 1 teaspoon dried elecampane root
- Small cauldron or other fire-proof dish
- Sand
- Self-igniting charcoal
- Long-reach lighter or long-reach matches
- Photo(s) of missed friends/family/place
- Several small sheets of paper

Instructions:

Light the candle and place your photo(s) on the altar or other working space.

Pour enough sand into the cauldron to make a half-inch layer. Place the charcoal in the center and light one edge with the long-reach lighter or match. Once it sparks, leave it to self-ignite across the surface.

Carefully place the elecampane root in the center of the charcoal.

Take a few moments to visualize yourself spending time with someone you miss. What are the characteristics that you appreciate most about this person? Identify at least three memories involving this person that make you smile every time you recall them. Finally, what do you like about yourself when you are with this person—in other words, what qualities do they bring out in you?

Now, write down at least six things that came to mind, whether these are qualities or specific memories about the person.

Fold the paper in half three times. Waft the paper through the smoke, but do not let it ignite.

Say these words each time it passes through,

"We will always be together, whether near or far. I allow this spell to brighten my heart."

Repeat with each person—or place—you're missing, until your heart feels light and your sadness has passed.

You can send your loved ones the notes from your visualization if you wish, or keep them for yourself as magical mementos.

ELECAMPANE DIVINATION TEA

Traditionally, elecampane has a strong association with what some called "other-kind": elves, faeries and elemental spirits. Many people have experienced a stronger connection with the "Otherworld" in general—be it spirit guides, angels, deities, or whatever one personally connects to for guidance and advice—when drinking an infusion of elecampane root prior to or during divination activities.

On its own, elecampane tea is quite bitter, so you'll likely only want to use 1/4 teaspoon of the cut root and sweeten the tea with plenty of honey.

If your divination is related to a specific question or area of your life, you might choose a corresponding candle color, such as red or pink for love, or green or brown for abundance. Black, white and violet are associated with divination in general, so these make great choices as well.

<u>You will need:</u>

- Pillar candle (any color)
- ¼ teaspoon plus additional pinch of elecampane root
- Honey
- Tea strainer (optional)
- Tarot deck, oracle cards or runes
- Journal or writing paper (optional)

<u>Instructions:</u>

Prepare the tea, saving a pinch of the elecampane root for an offering to the faeries.

Steep the tea for 3 to 5 minutes, strain out the root, and sweeten to taste with the honey.

Light the candle and spend a few moments quieting your mind as you sip your tea.

When you feel ready to begin your divination, take the pinch of elecampane root and sprinkle it over the candle so that at least some of it lands on the flame (but not enough to extinguish the candle).

Say the following (or similar) words:

"I welcome the wisdom of the spirit world, and thank my guides for their presence at this time."

Now, begin your divination.

Write down any significant messages for later reference.

The candle may be gently extinguished and used again for divination at a later time.

SACHET FOR OPENING YOUR HEART TO LOVE

Sometimes we can be damaged by past relationships, be they destructive or just disappointing. Even after we recover from initial heartbreak, fear can leave us closed off to new possibilities for love, ultimately leading to a stagnant or stuck place when it comes to moving on.

On the one hand, we may want to reach out for new connections, but on the other we are still rather closed off. But love always involves an element of risk, so if you want a new relationship, you'll need to be willing to let go of lingering fears.

Elecampane is a powerful herb for openings, both physically and spiritually. This spell can help you open yourself up to the new possibilities that are always just around the bend, regardless of what seems possible at the moment.

<u>You will need:</u>

- Pink candle
- Elecampane flowers
- Pink cloth
- Needle and pink thread

<u>Instructions:</u>

Place the elecampane flowers, cloth, needle, and thread on your table or altar.

Take some time to sit quietly and breathe deeply.

As you breathe in, imagine a bright white light filling your body.

As you exhale, imagine all stress, tension and any emotional pain leaving your body, allowing more and more space for the light from the next inhale to come in.

Light the candle, focusing your intention on allowing love to enter your life.

Place the flowers on the cloth and fold it into a neat bundle or sachet.

Using the needle and pink thread, sew the cloth closed along the edges and sides.

As you sew, see each stitch representing the possibility of love entering and growing in your life. There is an endless number of stitches possible, just like there is endless potential in your life (and in yourself) for love.

When you have finished sewing, place the sachet in front of the candle while saying the following (or similar) words:

"Spirit of elecampane, open my heart.
Release all pain and grant me fresh start.
So let it be."

Leave the candle to burn out on its own.

Carry the sachet with you in your purse, or keep it in a space where you will see it often and be reminded to keep your heart open to new love.

ANTI-GOSSIP WORKPLACE PROTECTION SPELL

The energy of gossip is inherently negative, as it feeds on our lower vibrational frequencies and ultimately creates an atmosphere of general distrust. In the workplace, gossip disrupts efficient teamwork and sabotages what might otherwise be an enjoyable working environment. This spell helps keep the vibrational energy of your workplace free from the human tendency toward gossip.

Of course, if you are one of the gossipers (and most of us have been, at one time or another!), then the spell will not be effective. Be conscientious about ridding yourself of this destructive habit first, and then you will be energetically ready to protect the entire workplace, for your own peace of mind as well as that of your colleagues.

Since it may not be possible to physically walk around your place of employment in a meditative state sprinkling herbs on the ground, this spell is designed to be worked remotely from your home—but if you're able to do it at your actual workplace, all the better! If working remotely, prepare around your actual workplace a day or two before the spell. Observe as many small details as you can, building up in your mind a clear and detailed image of the space you will be focusing your magic on.

You will need:

- 1 teaspoon elecampane petals or powdered elecampane root
- Paper and pencil (if working remotely)
- Black candle

Instructions:

Light the candle, and draw a floor plan of your workplace on the paper. Don't worry about getting all the correct proportions or drawing completely straight lines—simply create a visual representation of the place, allowing your imagination to fill in the details.

Now, in your mind (or literally, if you're able to work the spell in person), "walk" the perimeter of the area that you want to protect from gossip.

As you walk, sprinkle elecampane petals or the powdered herb along the perimeter.

Visualize the sprinkled herb creating a protective barrier against negative words. See the barrier bounce the words back from where they came, not allowing any negativity inside.

When you have completed walking the perimeter, take a moment to visualize all the gossip flowing out of the area which you have protected.

When you have completed your visualization, drop a small a pinch of the elecampane petals or powdered root onto the candle flame. Save any unused elecampane to use again when you need to reinforce the barrier between you and negative gossip.

HIBISCUS

This lovely plant with its large, trumpet-like flowers is actually part of an extensive family—there are over 200 species of Hibiscus. The one we are most familiar with in Western culture is the tropical hibiscus. This beautiful equatorial plant, associated with the planet Venus, has been linked with all things feminine for thousands of years.

In Hindu worship, the hibiscus is an offering to both the powerful Goddess Kali, known for the ferocity of her love for her children as well as her ferocity in battle. A Hawaiian woman who wears a hibiscus in her hair is signaling her availability for marriage, according to which side she wears the flower on.

In Greek, the name is hibiscus rosa-sinesis, or "rose of china." In Singapore, it is called bunga raya, or "flower of celebration." In the Indian traditional system of medicine, Ayurveda, hibiscus is used in multiple concoctions to cure a variety of ailments including hair loss, anemia and skin inflammation. Today, the tea has become popular as a way of boosting vitamin C, aiding digestion, and healing the liver.

In ancient Egypt, hibiscus tea was actually forbidden to women because of its ability to induce lust. Wiccans and other magical folk have also noted this tendency, and have used hibiscus in spells to bring on passion, love and lust.

Associated with the Element of Water, hibiscus is also excellent for gently encouraging inner sight and strengthening clairvoyance. The petals are particularly good for scrying—the art of looking for images in water or on other surfaces to gain answers to questions and insight into the future.

Because hibiscus strengthens psychic abilities, it is an attractant to good spirits and a protection against negativity and malevolence. The following spells will show you to how to use hibiscus to try your hand at scrying, reconnect with your inner self, attract romantic love, and restore balance to your feminine side—no matter what your gender.

FLOWER-PETAL SCRYING BOWL

This spell uses the watery properties of hibiscus to strengthen your natural powers to see beyond that which you normally perceive with sight, sound, smell, taste and touch.

If you perform this scrying ritual regularly, you will begin to notice patterns and meaning that you did not see at first. To get the most out of this work, record your impressions in writing, even if you think they are unimportant or nonsensical at the time.

You will need:

- Handful (approximately ¼ cup) hibiscus flower petals
- Wooden bowl
- Water
- 2 white votive candles
- Journal or writing paper

Instructions:

Begin by visualizing a sphere of white light surrounding you and your magical space.

State your intention that only messages from positive, beneficent energies will be received.

Spend a few moments quieting your mind.

When you are ready, place the wooden bowl in the middle of your altar, on a table, or on the floor.

Light each votive candle and place it on either side of the bowl.

Extinguish all other lights so that only the candles remain.

Pour in the water until it reaches close to the top of the bowl and sprinkle the hibiscus leaves on the surface of the water.

Sit quietly and allow the water to begin to settle as you breathe. Inhale and count to four, then exhale and count to four. Close your eyes and repeat this process until you begin to feel very relaxed.

State the purpose of your magical work out loud. You might say, for example, "*It is my will to see the best way forward regarding my situation.*"

If you'd like to scry in a more general way, just to see what you will see, you might say something like, "*Love and light, Blessed Be. Show me what I need to see.*"

Allow yourself to gaze into the bowl of water as your eyes and mind relax. Let various images arise in the water and petals. Do not judge the images, or try to explain them. Just observe and let them flow into your vision.

When you feel you are done, record your experiences and thoughts in your journal.

PEACEFUL WHOLENESS AND WELL-BEING BATH SPELL

We all know that "me time" is important for refreshing our hearts, spirits and bodies. Here's a gloriously relaxing spell you can do with minimal preparation, in the comfort of your home, surrounded by the cheering essence of hibiscus as you re-connect with your larger self and sense of wholeness.

Note: depending on the type of tub you have, loose hibiscus flowers may leave a stain, though this usually washes away after a shower or two. You may want to test a small area with a wet hibiscus flower first. Use a mesh bag or cheesecloth if you're concerned about staining, and be sure to use a strainer to keep your drain clear when draining the tub afterward.

You will need:

- 2 tablespoons hibiscus petals
- Sea salt, Epsom salt, or other bath salts
- Indigo or deep blue candles
- Mesh bag or cheesecloth (optional)

Instructions:

Place the indigo candles around the bathroom and bathtub and light them.

Turn on the water and run a warm bath.

While the bath water is running, allow yourself to just be. Focus on the light from the candles, hear the running water, feel the warmth of the room, and allow yourself to begin to feel more connected to things around you.

When the water is ready, place the hibiscus petals in the bath while stating, *"I am whole. I am connected to everything around me and throughout the Universe."*

Step into the bathtub and allow yourself sink down into the warm water.

Meditate on what is harmonious and peaceful about yourself. Remain still and quiet, and simply be.

When you are ready, emerge from the tub, dry off, and blow out the candles.

Take this amazing feeling of wholeness with you throughout your day, or enjoy a peaceful night's rest.

IGNITE YOUR LOVE LIFE SPELL

This fun spell combines the passionate energy of hibiscus with the spark of the Element of Fire. Do use caution, as with any time you put your fingers in the vicinity of a candle flame.

If you can't find dried hibiscus leaves, look for dried petals large enough to be pinched between your fingers as you hold them to the flame, without burning yourself! Make sure the bowl is large enough to accommodate several smoldering leaves at once.

You will need:

- Heat-proof bowl
- 14 large dried hibiscus leaves (or very large petals)
- Red spell candle
- Pink spell candle
- Journal or writing paper

Instructions:

Place the red candle and the pink candle on either side of the small dish and light each one.

Take a moment to visualize a warm light swirling in pink and red around you. This is the light of attracting love and courage, strength and friendship—key qualities in any relationship.

Now make a list of 14 qualities and characteristics that you would like to attract in a partner. Divide the list up so that 7 of the qualities are more associated with the color red (passion, lust, courage, energy, etc.), and 7 are more related to pink (friendship, love, compassion, partnership, etc.). Don't overthink this, though, or try for perfect symmetry—just go with your gut.

Choose a quality from the "red" list, and then carefully ignite a dried hibiscus leaf using the red candle. Drop the leaf into the dish and say, *"I now bring a lover with [name the quality]."*

Now do the same with the "pink" list, only say "*partner*" in place of "*lover*" when you drop the ignited leaf.

Continue to alternate between the red and pink candles, placing each leaf or petal in the dish, until you have ignited each leaf.

Allow the hibiscus to smolder until it goes out on its own, and allow the candles to burn out on their own. When the ashes and bowl have cooled completely, bury the ashes in your yard.

DIVINE FEMININE INNER GODDESS RITUAL

At first glance, this spell may appeal more to women than men, but it's actually appropriate for all genders. We all have masculine and feminine aspects, and these two energies can become imbalanced in a fast-moving, action-oriented world.

In Western society, men and women often find that they're expected to stifle their emotions, rush from moment to moment without taking time for reflection, and prioritize material gains over spiritual needs. While the energy of the masculine certainly serves a vital role, too much of it leaves people (and the planet) depleted and out of balance.

The hibiscus flower, always associated with femininity and beauty, is a potent visual and spiritual reminder of the divine feminine. Here it helps you to realize, remember, appreciate and celebrate all the wonderful aspects of yourself that reflect the divine feminine.

<u>You will need:</u>

- Floating candle
- Bowl, cup or small cauldron of water
- 2 teaspoons dried hibiscus petals
- Journal or writing paper

<u>Instructions:</u>

Place the floating candle in the water and set the journal or paper in front of you. Light the candle and take a few moments to quiet your mind.

When you feel ready, sprinkle some of the petals into the water surrounding the candle.

Sprinkle most of the rest around and over the writing paper and say the following (or similar) words:

"As above, so below,
the Goddess dwells within.
I proudly connect my heart and soul
with the divine feminine."

Now, reflect on any experiences you've had, either recently or further back in time, where you felt the feminine qualities within you either repressed or rejected by others.

For women, this may take the form of overt sexism. For men, it may have been a time when speaking from your heart would have been extremely taboo. Whatever the experience was, now is an opportunity to balance that energy by allowing your true feminine side to be expressed.

Write about the experience(s), identifying whatever it was that was rejected or repressed in the past.

Now re-imagine this experience in a way that allows you to express that feminine energy with a full sense of sovereignty, connected to your whole self. See yourself saying what it is you wanted to say, or doing what you wish you had done. Rewrite the story on the paper and cross out the original version.

Fold the paper 13 times (the number of the Divine Feminine) and waft it through the candle smoke, repeating the above words. Then bury the paper in your yard and sprinkle the remaining hibiscus petals over the spot.

LAVENDER

Native to the Mediterranean region, lavender has been utilized for medicinal, magical and even domestic purposes across many cultures for thousands of years. For example, Roman soldiers used the wild-growing herb to wash their clothes and perfume their bathwater. This continued into the Middle Ages, when washer women were called "lavenders."

A member of the mint family, this alkaline plant has antiseptic and astringent properties. Lavender pastilles were popular for decades throughout Europe as a breath freshener. Applying lavender oil to a wound can increase cellular growth, with the dual effect of speeding up the healing process and decreasing the appearance of scars.

Lavender's chemical properties appeal to our intellect; its heady aroma can transport us to a calmer mind, or to pleasant memories of childhood. Whether it's used for medicine, aromatherapy, or magic, lavender is one of the most soothing herbs you can find.

Magically, lavender is a masculine herb, associated with the planet Mercury and the element of Air. Witches often use lavender as an asperging herb, dipping the plant in water and sprinkling it around the ritual space for purification before beginning a spell.

It is also useful in dried form, and lavender sticks make a potent incense that brings about calmness of mind and discourages malevolent spirits from entering into a space. In some cultures, lavender is traditionally thrown into bonfires to drive away evil spirits, or strewn on the floors of churches to similar effect.

Lavender can be used for a multitude of other magical purposes, including healing, divination, peaceful sleep, consecration of ritual tools and attracting money. Due to the association with Air, lavender is wonderful when a spell is needed to sharpen the mind in matters of effective communication with others. Finally, lavender is useful in love magic, for spells attracting pure love or strengthening long-term love.

In this chapter, you will learn how to use lavender in spells for healing, sharpening your mental acuity, strengthening pure, soulful love, and sleeping better than you have in ages.

MIND-SHARPENING SPELL

Whether you're in school, training for a job, or simply wanting to clear up a case of "brain fog," this spell will help you increase concentration, boost your learning ability, and improve memory.

The calming properties of lavender promote clarity of mind, in part by reducing the mental clutter that is so prevalent in the midst of our noisy modern world. The color yellow, associated with the Element of Air, also corresponds to mental acuity.

<u>You will need:</u>

- Several sprigs of flowering lavender
- Yellow ribbon or thread
- Yellow candle

<u>Instructions:</u>

Take a few deep breaths, inhaling the deep relaxing scent of fresh lavender as you release any negative thoughts.

Light the yellow candle.

Gather the sprigs of lavender and bind them together in a small bouquet using the yellow ribbon.

As you wind the ribbon around the sprigs, visualize yourself completing your learning task—whether it's a class, a job, or anything else—with satisfaction and pride in your abilities. If any other thoughts creep in during your visualization, let them quickly pass through and disappear out of your mind.

Use a few drops of wax from the yellow candle to seal the ribbon or thread around the bouquet.

Hold the bouquet in your hands and say the following (or similar) words:

"Power of lavender, bright bouquet
Mental clutter is swept away
Yellow of East, yellow of air
My mind is now sharp and clear."

Hang the bouquet from your desk or from the ceiling near your desk or study area. You can also keep it in a desk drawer at work, if you're not comfortable with it being seen.

PURE-LOVE ENERGY LAVENDER OIL

Although lavender oil can certainly be used in love spells, the focus for this particular ritual is not romance, but rather the pure essence of love as a Universal energy. Pure love is the magical, divine state of being that is proof that goodness exists in the world, that we can relate to each other in compassion, and that peace is possible.

If we allow it, pure love can infuse every moment of every day, and when we see with truly loving eyes we make the world a better place. Pure love is powerful, creative, and the force in the world from which all good arises.

Use the following working when negative feelings threaten to overwhelm you, when you feel yourself losing touch with the joy of connecting to other people, or when you find yourself judging others and yourself harshly. You can use the oil all at once or save some for another working—you'll just need a small glass jar with a screw-top lid to store it in.

Lavender essential oil—unlike the dried herb, which has a fairly light and mild scent—is very potent, so use it sparingly in blends until you get a sense of how much you can enjoy without getting overwhelmed.

You will need:

- Small bowl
- 1/8 cup (or 2 tablespoons) carrier oil (such as olive, grapeseed or almond oil)
- 3-5 drops lavender essential oil
- Pink candle

Instructions:

Take some time to breathe deeply and quiet your mind. Open the lavender oil and very lightly inhale the scent.

Light the candle and visualize a state of peacefulness, where all is well and nothing needs to be judged as "good" or "bad." Imagine yourself free of all resentments toward yourself or others.

Pour the carrier oil into the bowl and slowly add the lavender oil, one drop at a time. Swirl the oils together after each drop.

When you've added enough lavender oil, give the bowl a final swirl and then hold it in both hands.

Concentrate on the feelings of pure love and charge the oil by saying the following (or similar) words:

"Pure light, pure love,
as below, so above.
I am connected to all that is
through pure love.
So let it be."

When you have finished your visualization, use the oil to anoint your skin, infusing your body with the loving energies of lavender.

Apply the oil whenever you feel the desire to surround yourself with pure love.

A MIND-BODY HEALING BATH SPELL

When it comes to healing from any illness or injury, one's state of mind is absolutely crucial—after all, the power of our thoughts is what creates our reality. When illness or injury begins to bring you down emotionally, use the following spell to enhance your ability to relax, so that your mind can work in tandem with your body to hasten your recovery.

Allowing the lavender flowers to float loose in the water can be a lovely experience, but you may want to place them in a mesh bag or cheesecloth if you don't have a strainer to keep your drain clear after the bath.

You will need:

- Loose lavender flowers
- 3-5 drops lavender essential oil
- White candle
- Mesh bag or cheesecloth (optional)

Instructions:

Run a warm bath to begin the ritual.

When the tub is full, light the white candle and add the lavender flowers and oil, saying the following (or similar) words:

"The spirit of lavender heals my mind and body and nourishes my soul."

Turn off all artificial lighting and enter the bath.

While you are in the water, focus on your breathing and on each exhale, visualize the illness releasing from your body and dissipating into the air.

As you breathe in, visualize the warm, lavender water strengthening your body and providing sustenance to your soul.

When you are ready, drain the bath, discard the lavender, and gently extinguish the candle.

LAVENDER
GOOD NIGHT SLEEP SPELL

For those who deal with sleep issues, whether it's insomnia, restlessness, frequently waking up, or difficulty getting to sleep, this spell can make a huge difference. Lavender is calming on all levels—physical, emotional, spiritual and ethereal—making it one of the best-suited herbs for sleep magic. Essential oil of lavender is particularly helpful for inducing sleep.

Silver is associated with the Moon, with dreams and dreaming, and with the restful, waning phase of the lunar cycle.

You will need:

- Small pillow with pillowcase
- Several sprigs of fresh lavender
- Lavender essential oil
- Silver candle

Instructions:

Light the silver candle and take several deep breaths.

With each inhalation, bring tranquility, quiet, and calmness into your mind, and on each exhalation, release tension, worry, and frustrations.

Place the lavender sprigs, one at a time, inside the pillowcase.

As you insert each one, visualize yourself having a peaceful night of sleep with calm dreams.

When you're finished, place three drops of lavender essential oil on the pillow case and say the following (or similar) words three times:

"I sleep soundly, safely, deeply throughout the night.
All is well, all is right."

Again, focus your attention on the silver candle and your breathing.

Take three more deep breaths, this time relaxing your body to prepare for sleep.

Be sure to extinguish the candle before falling asleep.

Lie down and close your eyes, inhaling the calming scent of lavender, ready for a deep and relaxed slumber.

MUGWORT

Mugwort is a member of the daisy family and is known by many colorful names including wild wormwood, felon herb, St. John's plant, moxa, naughty man and sailor's tobacco.

The historical legends around mugwort are many. Anglo-Saxon Britons believed that mugwort was the most effective cure for "elf shot," a condition widely applied to anyone who became ill without obvious cause—the illness was blamed upon the invisible arrows of the Fae (faeries and elves).

It is known as St. John's plant due to the medieval belief that a girdle of the herb was worn by John the Baptist during his time in the wilderness. From this belief arose superstitions that wearing mugwort protected a traveler from sunstroke, exhaustion, wild animals and evil spirits.

In Holland and Germany it is believed that if you gather St. John's Plant on St. John's Eve (the Summer Solstice), you will be protected against disease and bad luck. In China, bunches of mugwort are hung in the home to protect against evil spirits during the Dragon Festival, and in Japan the herb is burned specifically to drive away the spirits of disease.

In Anglo-Saxon traditional witchcraft, mugwort is one of the nine sacred herbs, and is used at the start and the end of rituals to sanctify the ritual space, asserting the sacred nature of the working. Among Witches in general, mugwort is one of the most popular herbs for ritual incense and for smudging.

Considered magically feminine in nature, mugwort is associated with both Venus and the Moon, although its Elemental association is Earth. Mugwort is considered a sacred herb of Artemis, the Greek goddess of the Moon, which gives it its scientific name—*artemisia vulgaris*. Many magical traditions associate mugwort with divination, and some Witches use an infusion of mugwort to ritually cleanse their ritual and divination tools.

A powerful herb for dreaming, mugwort can be used to both bring about and balance out intense dreams. You will find a spell below to encourage lucid dreaming, as well as spells for repelling unwanted energies, enhancing divination, and protecting yourself during travel.

SACRED-SPACE ASPERGING RITUAL

Asperging is a time-honored method of using the Element of Water to ritually cleanse and bless a space. In this ritual, the space in question is your sacred space.

Whether you keep a permanent altar or have to set it up for each ritual or magical occasion, you most likely have a specific place for your practice—a bedroom, living room, or other space. The energies of mugwort are especially well-suited to remove unwanted energies and protect your magical sacred space.

<u>You will need:</u>

- Black candle
- Chalice or bowl of water
- Several sprigs of mugwort
- Deep blue ribbon

<u>Instructions:</u>

Light the candle.

Gather the mugwort sprigs into a bundle and tie the stems tightly together with the ribbon.

Holding the bundle over the candle (but not close enough to singe the herbs), say the following (or similar) words:

"Any unwelcome thing, be it visible or non,
will through this ritual cleansing soon be gone.
So let it be."

Now, holding the chalice or bowl in one hand, and the mugwort bundle by the stem end in the other, gently dip the leaves into the water.

Walk around the perimeter of the space, in a counter-clockwise direction (or widdershins), flicking the mugwort bundle so that it sprinkles the water onto the floor.

When you have finished, pour the water out onto the Earth. You can bury the mugwort, or remove the ribbon and toss the bundle onto a hearth fire or bonfire.

SMOKY DIVINATION SPELL

This spell is designed to make use of the smoke from mugwort incense and the flickering flame of a charged candle in order to divine answers to a specific question. However, if you'd like to personalize it by using a different form of divination (such as Tarot, runes, or a pendulum), then the incense and candle can be energetic adjuncts to the work.

For this ritual in particular, it is especially important to spend time quieting your mind, in order to be in a receptive mode for images and messages to come through. The scent of the burning mugwort will aid this process immensely, but it's still up to you to clear your mind of any daily distractions.

Above all, when you perform this ritual, believe in the possibilities. With practice, it is easier and easier to enter into a state in which the "third eye" is opened, and insight, intuition and divine messages can flow into your consciousness.

<u>You will need:</u>

- Mugwort incense

- Black candle
- Journal or writing paper

Instructions:

Set the incense and burner next to the candle.

Light the incense, and take a few moments to center your intentions for the divination—a single topic or issue for which you would like to reveal information.

Breathe deeply and inhale the scent of the mugwort.

Hold the candle in both hands and send your intentions for the divination directly into the wax.

When you feel ready, light the candle and say the following (or similar) words:

"Smoke of mugwort, swirling free
show me what I need to see."

Close your eyes and clear your mind once again.

Now open them and gaze softly at the smoke from the incense as it rises above your altar. Don't try to make any specific images appear—let them come as they will.

Allow the movements of the candle flame and any visible smoke from the candle to join the "conversation." You may need to allow for several minutes before you images or other information begins to emerge.

Write down any insights, images, or other notions to reflect upon over the coming days.

SAFE TRAVEL SPELL FOR LONG JOURNEYS

Peace of mind at the start of a journey, especially a long journey, is essential to an enjoyable trip. This spell draws on the ancient Romans' tradition of putting mugwort in their shoes before a long journey.

You won't need many ingredients for this spell, so it's perfect to be done before retiring early the night before your travels.

Note: if you're traveling internationally, check the customs regulations of the country you're entering, as some countries are quite strict about bringing in plant material across their borders.

<u>You will need:</u>

- Blue candle
- Pair of traveling shoes
- 2 sprigs of mugwort

<u>Instructions:</u>

Take four deep breaths to relax and focus—one for each direction on the compass.

Place the shoes you will wear the most on your travels on the altar (be sure the soles are clean first!).

Light the candle.

Hold the sprigs of mugwort in your hands as you visualize your shoes traveling across all the new places that you will explore. Visualize yourself safe and content in these places.

When you feel ready, place one sprig of mugwort in each of your shoes as you say the following (or similar) words:

"I walk in safety wherever I roam."

You can leave the sprigs in your shoes while you travel, or place them in your travel bag right before you leave. Either way, keep the sprigs with you to ensure safe journeys.

LUCID DREAM TEA

A lucid dream is one in which the dreamer can take control of the dream, at least for part of the time, without waking up, and without losing the feeling of the reality of the dream.

Lucid dreaming can allow the dreamer to change the tone of a nightmare, defeating monsters or escaping calamities. In a good dream, once you achieve lucidity you can "play," performing physically impossible feats that the waking realm would not allow, all within the safety of the subconscious.

Most people who can recall their dreams have accidentally experienced lucidity upon occasion. But developing a practice of vivid and lucid dreaming can be an incredibly powerful, and often fun, tool to enhance your life. The situations you encounter in these dreams can often be used to analyze issues and challenges you're confronting in waking life.

Mugwort is widely known as a "lucid dreamer's herb," and has been used in many shamanic cultures where it is native. However, it's important to note that unlike in our Western culture, where we have been conditioned to expect immediate results, those who work shamanically with plants know that a skill like lucid dreaming takes time to develop. Therefore, have patience with this spell, and be willing to practice it a few times before deciding whether or not lucid dreaming is for you.

Note: don't overdo it with this one, as large amounts of mugwort or prolonged use is not recommended. If you are pregnant or nursing, it is not safe for you to ingest mugwort at all.

<u>You will need:</u>

- 1 to 1 ½ teaspoons dried mugwort
- Tea strainer
- Mug
- Journal or writing paper

Instructions:

Before the ritual, make a cup of hot mugwort tea. Steep for 8 to 10 minutes as you get ready for bed, then strain out the mugwort.

Place the journal or paper (and pen) where you are able to write if you wake in the middle of the night, or once you wake in the morning.

When you are ready for bed, begin the ritual.

As you sit in bed, begin to take deep relaxing breaths.

Sip your mugwort tea as you focus your intention for your dreams. Are you looking for a solution to a problem, to gain more information, or a deeper understanding of an issue or situation in your life? It's important to focus your energy on a single intent in order to get a clear message in your dreams.

When you're clear on your intention, say the following (or similar) words:

"I openly welcome all opportunities to gain wisdom in the dream world."

Once you have finished your tea, quietly curl into bed and fall asleep.

When you wake, write down anything you can remember from your dream—especially the appearance of any numbers, names, animals, or anything else that seems unusual and significant. Keep these notes and refer back to them over the coming days and weeks.

NUTMEG

One of the most pleasantly aromatic herbs used in magic, nutmeg is actually a seed, or kernel, of the fruit from the Myristica fragrans tree. The shell of the same seeds yields the herb mace. Nutmegs are evergreen trees, native to the rainforest of the "Spice Islands" of Indonesia. Since antiquity, nutmeg has been highly prized for its aromatic, aphrodisiac and medicinal uses.

Nutmeg has a long tradition of helping with a variety of medicinal needs, including being carried to ward off boils, neuralgia, rheumatism and cold sores. Since ancient times, nutmeg and its oil were being used in Chinese and Indian traditional medicines for illnesses related to the nervous and digestive systems. Nutmeg encourages the appetite and aids in digestion. **A brief word: nutmeg should be used cautiously, as ingesting large amounts can cause hallucinations; pregnant women should not use nutmeg medicinally at all.**

Nutmeg is a masculine herb, associated with the Element of Air (and sometimes Fire) and the planet Jupiter. It is a potent ingredient for any magic, but particularly spells having to do with luck and positive feelings in general. Witches have been known to borrow from other magical traditions such as North American Hoodoo, where nutmeg is prized for its power to bring good luck in games of chance, and will carry whole nutmegs in a pocket or drill holes in them to make nutmeg amulets.

In many Wiccan traditions, nutmeg is frequently burned to bring luck, not only in games of chance, but for luck in the courtroom. In addition, nutmeg helps with divination, as well as enhancing perception and helping to see what is below the surface of a given situation.

Nutmeg is also, of course, an herb in which cooking and magic meet. Traditional Western holidays feature nutmeg strongly in cooking, and its warm, inviting, aromatic presence not only makes for delicious food, but also imbues hearth and home with a cozy, loving feeling. This property can be harnessed through magic, with or without culinary assistance, as you will see in one of the spells below. Other magical goals addressed in this chapter are resolving arguments, pleasant journeys, and general good luck.

HERB AND FLOWER SPELL FOR CLEARING AN ARGUMENT

In any relationship, arguments arise often when communication fails. Even with the best of intentions, we can sometimes cease letting our needs be known, or listening to someone else's needs. The resulting misunderstandings can lead to tension and increasing arguments. Nutmeg aids in enhancing our perception—our ability to understand what's going on beneath the surface of a difficult situation.

This ritual will help to bring honesty into a relationship, release negative emotions, and provide strength for healthy communication between two people. The yellow candle symbolizes the power of air, the literal flow of conversation. The rose petals add in a symbol of love, serving as a reminder that, with love and care, arguments can be solved and harmony restored to a relationship. This spell is useful in any relationship, be it a romantic partner, family member or friend.

<u>You will need:</u>

- Yellow candle
- Olive oil
- Pinch of dried mint
- Pinch of dried nutmeg
- Dried yellow rose petals
- Mortar and pestle or small bowl
- A photo or other symbol of the person

Instructions:

Begin by visualizing a white light starting in your core and slowly radiating outward until you are enveloped by a protective white light.

Mix the herbs and petals together in the mortar or bowl, visualizing your personal power flowing into the ingredients.

Rub the candle with a kitchen oil and then roll it in the herb and flower mixture.

Place the photo or symbol on your altar. Light the candle as you chant the following (or similar) words:

"Air, our breath flowing free, let us speak in honesty."

Continue the chant six times as you concentrate on the photo of the other person.

After the chant, sit quietly and allow your body to release the negative emotions surrounding this person so that you will be able to communicate openly and honestly to them at your next encounter.

Allow the candle to burn out. Then say the following (or similar) words:

"Upon the next time we meet, allow us to speak open and honestly.
So mote it be."

LUCKY-SPICE CHARM NECKLACE

This simple charm is a pared-down version of a folk magic tradition found in North America and the Caribbean. It's particularly useful when there's a specific situation you could use some good luck with, whether it's a friendly game of chance or something more serious like a court case or job interview. But you can also just make one for the fun of it, charge it with general good luck energy, and then keep it handy for when the perfect occasion might arise!

Star anise seed pods, with their distinctive and easy-to-thread formations, add their lucky energies to that of whole nutmeg. You can make this a necklace, bracelet or anklet—whatever you prefer.

You will need:

- 1 whole nutmeg
- Small drill
- 2 whole star anise pods
- Length of string or thin ribbon

Instructions:

Drill a small hole through the nutmeg.

Thread it onto the ribbon or string.

Now thread one star anise onto the left side of the nutmeg and the other onto the right.

Tie a knot on the outside of each star anise so that the three spices won't slide around too much on the string, but will rather stay close to each other at the center of the necklace or bracelet.

As you work, visualize your hands imbuing the string and the spices with your personal power.

When you're finished, tie the charm around your neck, wrist or ankle and say the following (or similar) words three times:

"Lucky stars, lucky spice,
my fortune now is very nice!"

HOME SECURITY ENERGY CHARM

This spell is especially useful for households in times of transition or uncertainty—when looking for a job, for example, or even when looking for a new place to live. No matter what circumstances are up in the air for you, your ability to navigate the changing times can be optimized by keeping the energy in your home as positive as possible.

Similar to the way the smell of a holiday pie, well-spiced with nutmeg, will infuse a whole home with a sense of warmth and security, the threaded whole nutmegs in this charm will act to encourage faith and trust that all will work out in your favor. The candle draws on the Earth properties of the color brown, and its associations with bringing security to the home. Establishing this energetic vibration within your home provides you with a consistent means of replenishing your personal energy as you ride out the storm.

Remember to hang this charm out of reach of small children and pets, as its pleasant aroma may cause your little ones to want to see how it tastes. The string of nutmegs can be re-charged as needed to keep the energy of security strong within the home.

You will need:

- 9 whole nutmegs
- Small drill
- String or thick thread
- Brown candle

Instructions:

Light the candle and place the string and nutmeg on the table or altar in front of you.

Drill a small hole through each whole nutmeg. (This can be done prior to the spell if need be.)

Once all nine of the nutmegs have holes, begin by tying a knot large enough that the nutmeg will not slip off in the string or thick thread.

String each nutmeg while visualizing yourself surrounded by all you could possibly need in this world—food, water, love, good health, prosperity, etc.

Once all nine nutmegs have been strung, tie a knot at the bottom to prevent them slipping off of the string.

Hold the charm in your hands and infuse it with the energies of warmth and security and say the following (or similar) words:

"As these walls stand, as this roof shelters,
I trust I will have all I need, forever."

Lay the nutmeg charm out in front of the candle until the candle has burned all the way down.

Then hang the string somewhere in your home where you have tended to be most susceptible to fear of lack or fear of change.

GOOD LUCK AIR-TRAVEL SPELL

Anyone who flies regularly these days knows that the odds of all going smoothly are not supremely high—especially at holiday times and during inclement weather. This small charm paves the way for you to experience a hassle-free flight no matter the time of year.

The nutmeg tree is ruled by Jupiter, a planet associated with optimism and expansion. Jupiter plants are known to bring about relaxation and mental calm—an important state to be in to navigate any potential issues while traveling. Yellow is the chief color correspondence for the Element of Air, and is also associated with travel.

<u>You will need:</u>

- 1 whole nutmeg
- Yellow piece of cloth
- Thin yellow ribbon
- 1 yellow spell candle

<u>Instructions:</u>

Light the candle and spend a few moments quieting your mind.

Spread out the cloth and place the nutmeg in the middle, gently wrapping it into the fabric.

Pull up the cloth on all four sides and tie the ribbon to secure the nutmeg inside. Use scissors to cut off any excess fabric.

Hold the wrapped nutmeg in your hands and visualize yourself fully enjoying your flight experience. Then imagine walking out of the airport with your luggage, satisfied and ready for whatever awaits you.

Your visualization should be of a perfect trip —see everything working smoothly and your travels as safe and easy. Repeat this perfect journey in your mind as many times as you need.

Place the nutmeg bundle in front of the candle and say the following (or similar) words:

"With the ease and grace of a bird in flight,
every detail of my trip will be right.
So let it be."

Place the wrapped nutmeg in your pocket or purse when traveling.

If you begin to feel anxious or nervous for any reason, bring it out and hold it between your hands to help you realign with your positive, lucky energy.

ROSEMARY

An evergreen shrub native to the Mediterranean, rosemary is a strong and fragrant member of the mint family. If the weather is humid enough, rosemary puts out delicate blue flowers in the spring and summer seasons. This pungent herb's name comes from the Latin *rosmarinus*, meaning "dew of the sea."

Rosemary was a sacred herb in ancient Egypt, where it was used in embalming and burned as incense in temples. The Greeks considered rosemary sacred to the goddess Aphrodite, and you can see it depicted alongside her in many images from ancient times. They also used rosemary to guard against nightmares, and rosemary wood to make musical instruments.

In the Middle Ages, people wore rosemary around their necks to ward off the "evil spirits" that brought on the plague, and in France rosemary was burned in sick rooms and hospitals to purify the air. Rosemary branches were also woven into wreaths to be worn by brides at weddings, and these branches were a common and treasured gift to wedding guests throughout medieval Europe.

Magically, rosemary has many uses. It is still used primarily in relation to its purifying properties—not only to repel negative energies, but to actively attract positivity. In some traditions, it is thought to be able to summon elves and faeries. Associated with both the Sun and the Moon and the Element of Fire, rosemary is also used to encourage fidelity in relationships and dispel jealousy.

It enhances memory—both in terms of the brain and the heart—and one the most powerful uses for this herb is in workings for making oneself "unforgettable." Rosemary is also used for dream work and past life recall, as well as retaining youthful vitality.

In this chapter, you'll find spells for encouraging longevity in a relationship, success on school tests, and purification of body and mind.

RELEASING NAGGING THOUGHTS

The mind is a natural problem solver. In terms of basic survival, this is a good thing—we figure out how to eat, where to shelter, and how to stay out of danger. However, there are plenty of situations in life that we can't simply think our way out of. And if we don't keep obsessive thinking in check, we can actually keep a problem in place simply by continuing to focus on it.

This bath spell is perfect for ridding yourself of persistent thinking about any situation you can't actually solve at the present moment. Whether it's the need to find a new job, an interpersonal conflict, or even simple regret about something that happened in the past, rosemary's purifying powers can help you shed your unwanted attachment to the situation, allowing you some neutral space that will most likely end up helping you find a solution down the road.

Lavender oil adds its own purifying and soothing vibrations, while lemon oil adds a bright note to the energetic benefits of this bath. Of course, the cleansing powers of sea salt take the purification factor even higher.

If you're new to essential oils, it's best to stick with just 3 drops of each oil until you get a better sense of how potent your particular oils are, and how much you can tolerate.

<u>You will need:</u>

- 3-5 drops rosemary essential oil
- 3-5 drops lavender essential oil
- 3-5 drops lemon essential oil
- ¼ cup sea salt
- White candle

Instructions:

Run a warm bath to begin the ritual. Add the salt and the oils to your bath and gently swirl the water. Light the white candle and turn off any artificial lighting.

Gently enter the bath and breathe deeply, allowing the scent of the oils to envelop you. Take a few deep breaths, focusing only on your inhalation and exhalation.

When you feel your mind has quieted, allow the situation that you've been obsessing about to come to the forefront of your mind, and say the following (or similar) words:

"I release this situation,
in perfect love and perfect trust.
I trust the Universe for resolution,
knowing all will work out as it must."

Relax in the bath for at least 15-20 minutes.

When you're ready, drain the bath, but stay in the tub so the waters can pull any remaining energy from the situation that may be trying to stay with you.

As you go about the next few days, if you find yourself worrying about the situation again, repeat the above words to yourself.

You can also uncap your rosemary oil and gently inhale the aroma to help you clear your mind.

ROSEMARY SMUDGE FOR PERSONAL PURIFICATION

Rosemary's purification properties work on both the physical and the energetic levels. This spell acts like a psychic house cleaning, allowing your body and mind to release any build-up of residual, unwanted energy picked up throughout your busy days.

During the purification, if any unwanted thoughts come into your mind, acknowledge them and then allow them to pass and float away.

Don't hold onto any thoughts, positive or negative. Just allow the thoughts to enter and exit your mind.

As with candles, it's important to be reverent when extinguishing smudging herbs. Don't use water or smash the smoldering end of the smudge in order to put it out. Instead, allow the soil to gently absorb the heat until the embers are gone.

You will need:

- 1 rosemary smudge stick
- White candle
- Soil from a potted plant (optional)

Instructions:

Place the candle at the center of your table or altar and light it. Take a few moments to quiet your mind, using deep breaths.

Light the smudge stick from the candle.

Stand straight up and down with your feet spread slightly apart.

Holding the smudge stick, begin at the top of your head and slowly swirl the rosemary around to purify your energy. Gently and slowly move it clockwise around your entire body, passing it from hand to hand when necessary.

You may feel the need to spend more time in some areas of your body than others. Spend as much time as you need swirling the smudge stick in order to cleanse that section. Take all the time you need to feel the full release of unwanted energy.

End the smudging at the top of your head. Take three more deep breaths with a clear mind in order to fully purify yourself.

Take the smudge stick outdoors and gently extinguish it in the soil (or in the soil of a potted plant).

Repeat this ritual any time you need to purify and cleanse your own energy.

CONFIDENCE SPELL FOR TEST-TAKERS

This spell is great for students facing midterms or final exams, but can be used in any situation where memory recall is a crucial factor. Rosemary's power to enhance memory is combined with the energy of the color orange, associated with confidence.

You will be creating a beautiful visual reminder of your ability to master the material you're studying, to recall the information when needed, and to align your magical energy with the natural world in order to improve your mind and your life.

The best place for this ritual is in your home where you generally study or practice such as in a certain room or at your desk.

<u>You will need:</u>

- 3 sprigs fresh rosemary
- Small vase filled with purified water
- Orange candle

<u>Instructions:</u>

Spend a few moments quieting your mind. When you're ready to begin, light the orange candle.

Hold the vase in your hands and send your personal power into the water, energizing it for optimal effect of the spell.

Focus on the light of the flame for a few moments as you visualize yourself beginning the test.

Place one rosemary sprig in the vase. Now visualize yourself feeling confident and successful while taking the test.

Place the second sprig of fresh rosemary in the vase. Finally, visualize yourself completing the test, feeling good about your results.

Keep the vase of rosemary on your desk or in your study space.

Repeat the spell for each new test, or when you feel the energy of the water and rosemary beginning to wane.

SUN-AND-MOON RELATIONSHIP LONGEVITY SPELL

Whether we realize it consciously or not, ritual is very important to the longevity of a relationship. Any couple who has let the ritual of "date night" fade away into the past will almost certainly experience difficulty in their relationship at some point.

Here is a beautiful, heart-warming ritual for you to do with your partner any time you wish to reconnect with and appreciate each other.

Drawing on rosemary's association with remembrance and longevity, this working also incorporates the traditional magical symbolism of the Sun and the Moon, representing the divine union of the God and Goddess. Here they are represented by the gold and silver candles, embodying the male and female energies that exist within each of us, and the balancing of which is so essential to a long-term relationship.

You will need:

- 1 sprig rosemary
- Ceremonial cup or goblet (preferably purchased together or significant in some way to the couple) filled with purified water
- Small gold candle
- Small silver candle

Instructions:

Before the ritual, place the candles and the cup or goblet of water on the altar. Place the rosemary sprig next to the chalice.

Sit across from one another and hold hands. Take three deep breaths together. Relax and feel the warmth of each other's energy and love.

When ready, each of you should light one of the candles. The gold symbolizes the sun and the silver is for the moon.

Together hold the rosemary sprig and place it in the water. Swirl it in the cup clockwise three times. While swirling the rosemary repeat the following (or similar) words in unison:

"May our love be true and strong, our lives together long."

Both people should take a sip from the cup or goblet to solidify their desire.

Take turns sharing reasons why you decided to commit to your partner. The person speaking should hold the rosemary sprig. Take a sip of the water after each turn, alternating until you have finished the cup.

At the end of the ritual, gently extinguish the candles and give one another a warm embracing hug.

SAGE

Appreciated for its magical powers by everyone from medieval Europeans to Native Americans, this hardy member of the mint family has purple spiky flowers in the summer, but it is the leaves you will find most helpful for your magical purposes. Their scent, when rubbed, can send you into a calm, meditative, magical state of mind, as anyone who has ever used this herb in cooking can attest.

The ancient Romans believed that sage stimulated the brain and memory, and used sage to clean their teeth. It was used in the Middle Ages to treat fevers, liver disease and epilepsy. In England, it's long been used in a tea as an all-around health tonic, especially useful in treating sore throats and coughs.

In Chinese medicine, sage tea treats weakness of the digestive system and imbalances of the nervous system. Sage also has antibacterial properties, which have just recently been "discovered" in scientific studies of smudging—a practice engaged in by Native Americans for millennia—in which sage has been found to literally obliterate bacteria in the air.

Magically, sage is associated with the Element of Air and the planet Jupiter. It is used primarily in magic related to clearing away unwanted energies from both people, objects and places, gaining wisdom, and healing from the loss of loved ones. In fact, the word "sage" is derived from the Latin *salveo*, meaning "to heal" or "to salve," which may point to an ancient understanding of the connection between this herb and the wounds of grief.

Sage is also a helpful ingredient in protections spells and workings for longevity, as well as clearing the mind and opening up the third eye. Some also use sage in spells for fertility and luck. In this chapter, you will learn how to use sage for cleansing your ritual tools, working through grief, and tapping into your inner wisdom.

SAGE TEA LONGEVITY SPELL

For Witches who are closer to their Crone years than to their Maiden years, the idea of longevity begins to take on more importance. But no matter your age or gender, this spell affirms your intention to live a long, healthy and happy life.

On the physical level, sage is very beneficial for a number of health issues, particularly related to stress and anxiety. The calming effects of a tea drinking ritual already reduce stress levels, so adding both the physical and magical energies of sage really intensifies the intention here. The crystals listed below are also associated with longevity and add a lasting physical component to the spell.

You will need:

- 1 teaspoon dried sage leaves
- Tea strainer (optional)
- White candle
- 1 piece of amethyst, garnet, citrine or carnelian
- Journal or writing paper

Instructions:

Light the candle and brew the tea.

While it steeps, begin making a list of things in the distant future that you look forward to experiencing. This will depend on your current age, but could include retiring, traveling, becoming a grandparent, or anything else you envision happening a long way off from now.

When the tea is ready, sip it slowly and choose one of the items on your list. Write a description of this event or circumstance in the present tense—describe your travels, your grandchildren, or whatever it is you want to envision in more detail. Write about it as if it is happening right now.

When you're finished writing, fold the paper three times and set it under the candle holder (be sure the diminishing candle won't ignite the paper).

Take the crystal and dip it very quickly into the remainder of your tea.

Set it in front of the candle to dry.

Keep the crystal somewhere where you will see it often and remember your affirmation to live a long life.

CLEANSING RITUAL TOOLS AND MAGICAL OBJECTS

Just as places can accrue traces of energy from prior inhabitants and events, so too your ritual instruments can accrue "leftovers." Regularly keeping your tools physically and energetically clean will remove any chance of past energies clashing with your current ritual or magical intentions. Additionally, the very act of spiritually cleansing your tools is a meditative act that will encourage you to treat them with reverence, and therefore imbue them with your own pure energy.

Sage has been used for centuries in nearly every culture where it has grown to sanctify temples, cleanse ritual spaces, and purify the important implements and tools used in magical workings. Here, the incense is a bit more convenient than a full sage smudge stick, but either will work fine. If you do use a smudge stick, just be sure to have a fire-proof dish it can sit and smolder in.

You might like to use this working in tandem with the cinnamon anointing oil (page 53) using sage to clear the objects and the cinnamon oil to consecrate them.

<u>You will need:</u>

- Ritual/magical object(s) to cleanse
- Sage incense (or smudge stick) and holder
- Work candle for atmosphere (optional)

Instructions:

Light the candle, if using.

Place the object or objects you want to cleanse on your altar or table. Physically wipe off any dirt or dust.

Light the sage incense and wait for a tendril of smoke to form.

In order to disassociate the object with past vibrations, pass it through the smoke from end to end.

Once it has been cleansed, pass it through the smoke again from end to end in order to attune it with your own energies.

Repeat this with each object to be cleansed.

This spell can be repeated as necessary whenever you need to remove or replace energy in ritual or other personal objects.

CIRCLE OF LIFE RITUAL FOR HEALING GRIEF

Witches know that death is a natural part of the circle of life, and that grief is a healthy response to the loss of a loved one. The following ritual is a beautiful way to honor a loved one who has gone to the other side, while helping those still on the Earth plane to move through the healing process. Sage has long been known as an herb that soothes and comforts in times of deep grief.

As you enact this ritual, it is important to allow your feelings to flow. Take your time and let all the feelings that well up in you to be expressed, even if they surprise you or make you uncomfortable. This is part of the cleansing purpose of grief.

At the end of the ritual, you will share your grief with the Earth, the Great Mother. We are all children of the Earth, and as you focus on your feelings, you should feel a healing balm radiating up from the ground, reminding you that you are a part of the great spirit of life.

You will need:

- 3 large sage leaves
- Photo of your loved one
- Purple candle
- Writing paper and pen
- Envelope
- Spade

Instructions:

Light the candle and take a few moments to meditate on the person you have lost. Focus on memories that brought you joy and on characteristics and attributes of the person that you most admired.

When you feel ready, write a letter to the person. It can be as long or as short as you need. You can write in any style that fits you best. Allow your feelings to pour out onto the paper.

Once you feel finished, place the letter along with the sage leaves in the envelope.

Seal it with a few drops of melted wax from the candle, and leave the candle to burn out on its own.
Use the spade to bury the letter in a place that was special to you and that person.

Once you have buried the letter, place your hands on the mound and send your energy into the earth.

SAGE LEAF WISDOM SPELL

Sometimes there are issues or dilemmas that no amount of logic, problem-solving, or even divination attempts can shed any light on. For the truly big questions in life, the magical properties of sage can help you release any stuck energy caused by "spinning your tires" over a problem and open your sixth sense enough to receive guidance from the spirit realm.

This spell is best worked at night, shortly before going to bed. Often enough, the clues you're seeking will appear to you in your dreams.

<u>You will need:</u>

- 7-10 sage leaves
- Blue or black candle
- Journal or writing paper (optional)
- Work candle for atmosphere (optional)

<u>Instructions:</u>

Light the work candle, if using.

Spend some time in quiet meditation.

If you're feeling a lot of energetic charge around the situation—anxiety, emotional upset, etc.—you may want to do some freewriting about it in order to clear your mind.

Now, arrange the sage leaves so that they form a circle around the candle, keeping back at least one. Rub this one on your wrists and temples.

Begin speaking out loud to the Universe about your situation. Explain it as if speaking to a friend.

When you're ready, formulate the clearest question you can about the situation and ask it directly.

Then light the candle and say the following (or similar) words:

"I now release my question to the wise Crone energy of the Universe."

Allow the candle to burn out on its own.

Leave the sage leaves in place overnight, and bury them in the Earth the next day.

If the answers have not come to you yet, you will find that they do over the next few days.

THYME

This tiny-leafed garden herb is another member of the mint family, and has long been used to flavor soups, stews and other savory dishes. Historical records show that thyme has been in magical and medicinal use since ancient Egypt, where it was used along with rosemary as a rub before mummification, and in household use as a pain killer. Roman emperors particularly favored thyme, as they ate it before a meal to foil any poison attempts and also gave it to their soldiers before a battle as a sign of courage. Ancient Greek women wore thyme in their hair to increase their attractiveness.

Thyme's use as an antiseptic was recorded as early as 3000 BCE by Sumerians, and by the plague years of the Middle Ages, thyme was a common ingredient in many treatment and pain killing medicines. Essential oil of thyme, known as thymol, is still used as a disinfectant and an antiseptic, and modern herbalists have recommended thyme to treat sinus infections and freshen breath.

Magically, thyme is aligned with the feminine energies, the Element of Water, and the planets Mercury and Venus. Said to be a popular dwelling space for faeries, the plant has long been used to summon and communicate with the faerie realm—wild, fresh-picked thyme is worn as a charm, or the essential oil is used in order to open the eyes to the faerie realm and receive psychic knowledge.

Another association of thyme is with bringing about an increase in monetary fortune. Both "Three Jacks" and "King Oil," popular lucky oils used by gamblers, count thyme as a main ingredient, and folklore states that when we plant thyme in the garden, our money luck will increase as the thyme crop grows.

Practitioners of Wicca often burn thyme before rituals to magically cleanse the ritual area. It is also burned in spells for healing and for developing psychic powers, and can be carried to smell when courage and energy is needed. In this chapter, you will find spells using thyme for courage, confidence, resilience and abundant luck.

THYME COURAGE TALISMAN

This talisman is useful during periods of your life requiring extra courage. This could mean starting a new job, moving to a new town, dealing with a medical crisis, or any other life situation that feels daunting.

You will need:

- Several sprigs of dried thyme
- 8-10 inch length of orange ribbon
- Black construction paper
- Glue
- Hole punch
- Work candle for atmosphere (optional)

Instructions:

Light the candle, if using.

On the construction paper, trace a circle up to 3 inches in diameter, using the bottom of a cup or some other circular shape. Cut out the circle and punch a hole through the center.

One at a time, carefully glue the stem ends of the thyme sprigs to the circle so that at least some of the leaves hang over the circle's edge, creating a "mandala" effect.

Be intentional with your placement of the thyme and as you glue down each piece, visualizing yourself feeling strong and courageous.

When the glue has dried, take a moment to hold the talisman gently between your palms and visualize your energy and strength pouring into it.

Thread the ribbon through the hole and hang the talisman where you can see and touch it often.

When the situation you made it for has passed, bury it in the earth or toss it on a hearth or bonfire, giving thanks for its assistance in your time of need.

PENTAGRAM SELF-CONFIDENCE SPELL

It's probably fair to say that Witches are already a reasonably self-confident bunch, given the courage it takes to pursue such an unconventional path in life. Nonetheless, we all have our moments of self-doubt, especially when facing new challenges.

This spell serves as a nice reminder of your talents, skills, and other positive qualities, which you can summon up at your disposal as long as you remember who you are. Try this spell the next time you're feeling any doubt about your ability to accomplish a given goal.

You will be creating a pentagram (5-pointed star) with the thyme sprigs. You may want to draw or print out an image of a pentagram to help you with the placement of the thyme during the spell.

Although reds and oranges are traditionally associated with confidence, you should feel free to trust your intuition here and choose the color that resonates most with you.

<u>You will need:</u>

- 5 thyme sprigs
- Candle
- Pentagram image (optional)

<u>Instructions:</u>

Light the candle and spend a few moments quieting your mind.

Hold the first sprig and think of something that you are good at doing. Say out loud, *"I am good at_________,"* and place the sprig on the altar in front of the candle, leaving enough room to complete the star.

With the second sprig, think of a time that you showed kindness to another. Say out loud, *"I showed kindness to _________,"* and place the sprig on the altar to begin to create the pentagram.

With the third sprig, think of a time you overcame a challenge. Say out loud, *"I've shown that I can overcome _________,"* and place the sprig to continue the star.

With the fourth sprig, think of an attribute about yourself that you genuinely feel proud of. Say out loud, *"I take pride in my _________,"* and place the sprig to continue the star.

With the final sprig, think of something you're feeling challenged by at the moment. Say out loud, *"I know I can overcome _________,"* and place the sprig on the altar to complete the star.

Take a few deep breaths, allowing yourself to be filled with the energy of self-confidence.

Allow the candle to burn out on its own.

Crumble the thyme sprigs in your fingertips and scatter them out over the Earth.

RESILIENCE AND PROSPERITY PLANTING SPELL

Sometimes our plans simply don't pan out like we hoped they would. It can be all too easy to lose confidence at these times, whether we've lost a job, not won a scholarship we worked hard towards, or had to close down a failing business. Left too long, this loss of confidence can lead to despair and even apathy, keeping us closed off to whatever new opportunity the Universe is trying to present us with.

In addition to its magical associations with luck and prosperity, thyme is known as a hardy perennial, able to withstand cold temperatures by dying back and reemerging in the spring. Thus, it's a perfect plant to work with when you need to renew your optimism regarding a prosperity issue.

The physical results of this spell are quite literal, as you will be growing and tending to an entire thyme plant, continually reminding you that the end of one path leads to the beginning of the next. As you watch the lovely, aromatic plant being you are growing, you will be able to look forward to the future, knowing that every obstacle we face simply shifts our path toward a new, unexpected outcome.

This spell is ideally worked outdoors, but your altar or other workspace is fine, too—just be aware that potting plants can be messy!

<u>You will need:</u>

- Small thyme plant start (preferably organic)
- Small pot
- Potting soil (preferably organic)
- Water
- Green or gold ribbon (optional)

<u>Instructions:</u>

Take a moment to acknowledge the sadness around your loss, and any fear you may be experiencing because of it.

Then take a deep breath and on the exhale, release all attachment to this old vision for your life. Say the following (or similar) words:

"The past is behind me, and I gracefully close the door."

Now, place some soil into the pot. Hold the thyme gently in your hands and say the following (or similar) words as you position the root ball into the soil:

"In this present moment is the potential for vastly more."

Fill the remaining space in the pot with more soil, being sure that the roots are well covered, the base of the plant is exposed, and no more than 1/2 inch or so of space remains above the soil.

Now gently water your new plant, recognizing that nurturing this plant's growth will be like nurturing the next phase in your life—and will bring you luck in your next endeavor.

"With my positive intentions, new prosperity I ensure."

As it grows strong and healthy, your new plans will also grow strong and healthy.

If you like, tie a green or gold ribbon around the pot to add a little spark of color magic.

Put the plant in the sun either inside or outside.

Each time you water and tend to your thyme, know that you are growing new beginnings.

Inhale its scent for strength and positivity, and use the leaves (once it matures enough) in culinary and magical recipes.

LUCKY THYME INFUSED OIL

One of the most delightful uses for herbs in magic is some good old-fashioned kitchen witchery. Here, the magical intention for good money luck infuses olive oil that you can use on salads and pasta, boosting your receptivity to unexpected fortune.

One note of caution: any moisture retained by the herb will eventually spoil an infused oil. Be sure the thyme is completely dry before working this spell. To get the most flavor out of this process, choose an olive oil made from a blend of olives rather than from a single origin. (These are usually less expensive as well!)

<u>You will need:</u>

- 3-5 sprigs of dried thyme
- Canning jar or glass bottle with rubber stopper
- Mild olive oil

Instructions:

Gently "bruise" the thyme sprigs with your fingers to begin releasing their fragrance, but leave them whole—don't crumble them.

Place them in the jar (or bottle) and then hold it between your palms.

Visualize your personal energy charging the jar with the delight and joy you feel whenever you receive a boon of abundance—whether it be money, gifts, or simply beautiful weather on a special outdoor occasion.

Send that feeling into the jar and see the same energy emanating from the thyme.

Fill the jar with olive oil, being sure to thoroughly cover the sprigs.

Seal the jar and let it sit in a cool, dark place for 7 days.

Taste the oil, and if it's not infused strongly enough to your liking, leave for up to another 7 days.

When the oil is sufficiently infused with the thyme, use it to drizzle over salads, pasta, crusty bread, or anything else it goes well with.

If you won't be using it up within a few days, strain out the thyme and pour the oil into a new jar or bottle.

CONCLUSION

As you work more and more with herbal magic, you will develop a natural affinity with these marvelous plant beings that have been with magic users since the beginning of time.

As you expand your practice, if you find yourself overwhelmed by the possibilities, you might try an approach similar to the structure of this book. Simply "adopt" one or two new herbs at a time, working a few different spells with them before moving onto the next. Just be sure to research any herb you're unfamiliar with before using it for any purpose, to prevent any possibility of accidental harm due to toxicity.

And don't forget that books, online resources and herbal experts are not the only sources of information about herbs. The plant kingdom itself can communicate with you directly, if you'll only listen.

Enjoy following your path with herbal magic, and Blessed Be!

THREE FREE AUDIOBOOKS PROMOTION

Don't forget, you can now enjoy **three audiobooks completely free of charge** when you start a free 30-day trial with Audible.

If you're new to the Craft, *Wicca Starter Kit* contains three of Lisa's most popular books for beginning Wiccans. You can download it for free at:

www.wiccaliving.com/free-wiccan-audiobooks

Or, if you're wanting to expand your magical skills, check out *Spellbook Starter Kit,* with three collections of spellwork featuring the powerful energies of candles, colors, crystals, mineral stones, and magical herbs. Download over 150 spells for free at:

www.wiccaliving.com/free-spell-audiobooks

Members receive free audiobooks every month, as well as exclusive discounts. And, if you don't want to continue with Audible, just remember to cancel your membership. You won't be charged a cent, and you'll get to keep your books!

Happy listening!

MORE BOOKS BY LISA CHAMBERLAIN

Wicca for Beginners: A Guide to Wiccan Beliefs, Rituals, Magic, and Witchcraft

Wicca Book of Spells: A Book of Shadows for Wiccans, Witches, and Other Practitioners of Magic

Wicca Herbal Magic: A Beginner's Guide to Practicing Wiccan Herbal Magic, with Simple Herb Spells

Wicca Book of Herbal Spells: A Book of Shadows for Wiccans, Witches, and Other Practitioners of Herbal Magic

Wicca Candle Magic: A Beginner's Guide to Practicing Wiccan Candle Magic, with Simple Candle Spells

Wicca Book of Candle Spells: A Book of Shadows for Wiccans, Witches, and Other Practitioners of Candle Magic

Wicca Crystal Magic: A Beginner's Guide to Practicing Wiccan Crystal Magic, with Simple Crystal Spells

Wicca Book of Crystal Spells: A Book of Shadows for Wiccans, Witches, and Other Practitioners of Crystal Magic

Tarot for Beginners: A Guide to Psychic Tarot Reading, Real Tarot Card Meanings, and Simple Tarot Spreads

Runes for Beginners: A Guide to Reading Runes in Divination, Rune Magic, and the Meaning of the Elder Futhark Runes

Wicca Moon Magic: A Wiccan's Guide and Grimoire for Working Magic with Lunar Energies

Wicca Wheel of the Year Magic: A Beginner's Guide to the Sabbats, with History, Symbolism, Celebration Ideas, and Dedicated Sabbat Spells

Wicca Kitchen Witchery: A Beginner's Guide to Magical Cooking, with Simple Spells and Recipes

Wicca Essential Oils Magic: A Beginner's Guide to Working with Magical Oils, with Simple Recipes and Spells

Wicca Elemental Magic: A Guide to the Elements, Witchcraft, and Magical Spells

Wicca Magical Deities: A Guide to the Wiccan God and Goddess, and Choosing a Deity to Work Magic With

Wicca Living a Magical Life: A Guide to Initiation and Navigating Your Journey in the Craft

Magic and the Law of Attraction: A Witch's Guide to the Magic of Intention, Raising Your Frequency, and Building Your Reality

Wicca Altar and Tools: A Beginner's Guide to Wiccan Altars, Tools for Spellwork, and Casting the Circle

Wicca Finding Your Path: A Beginner's Guide to Wiccan Traditions, Solitary Practitioners, Eclectic Witches, Covens, and Circles

Wicca Book of Shadows: A Beginner's Guide to Keeping Your Own Book of Shadows and the History of Grimoires

Modern Witchcraft and Magic for Beginners: A Guide to Traditional and Contemporary Paths, with Magical Techniques for the Beginner Witch

FREE GIFT REMINDER

Just a reminder that Lisa is giving away an exclusive, free spell book as a thank-you gift to new readers!

Little Book of Spells contains ten spells that are ideal for newcomers to the practice of magic, but are also suitable for any level of experience.

Read it on read on your laptop, phone, tablet, Kindle or Nook device by visiting:

www.wiccaliving.com/bonus

DID YOU ENJOY *WICCA SPELLBOOK STARTER KIT*?

Thanks so much for reading this book! I know there are many great books out there about Wicca, so I really appreciate you choosing this one.

If you enjoyed the book, I have a small favor to ask—would you take a couple of minutes to leave a review for this book on Amazon?

Your feedback will help me to make improvements to this book, and to create even better ones in the future. It will also help me develop new ideas for books on other topics that might be of interest to you. Thanks in advance for your help!

CPSIA information can be obtained
at www.ICGtesting.com
Printed in the USA
LVHW041324110820
662814LV00004B/4

9 781912 715473